WESTMAR COLLEGE L

W9-AFL-188

MY DINNER
WITH ANDRÉ

ALSO BY WALLACE SHAWN
PUBLISHED BY GROVE PRESS

Marie and Bruce

MY DINNER WITH ANDRÉ

A Screenplay by

WALLACE SHAWN and ANDRÉ GREGORY

Grove Press, Inc./New York

PN
1997
.M89
1981

Copyright © 1981 by Wallace Shawn and André Gregory

All Rights Reserved

No part of this book may be reproduced, stored in a retrieval system, or transmitted in any form, by any means, including mechanical, electronic, photocopying, recording, or otherwise, without the prior written permission of the publisher.

CAUTION: This screenplay is fully protected, in whole, in part, or in any form, under the copyright laws of the United States of America, the British Empire including the Dominion of Canada, and all other countries of the Copyright Union, and is subject to royalty. All rights, including professional, amateur, stock, motion picture, radio, television, recitation, and public reading, are strictly reserved. All inquiries concerning professional and amateur rights should be addressed to the authors, in care of Grove Press, Inc., 196 West Houston Street, New York, N.Y. 10014.

First Evergreen Edition 1981
Third Printing—1982
ISBN: 0-394-17948-X
Library of Congress Catalog Card Number: 81-47639

Manufactured in the United States of America

GROVE PRESS, INC., 196 West Houston Street, New York, N.Y. 10014

101771

To my mother and father, Mary and Allen

—W.S.

For Lydia, my mother

—A.G.

Acknowledgments

The authors would like to thank

Suzanne Weil
Lyn Austin
Richard Avedon
Arthur Ballet
Gerry Bamman
James Bruce
Jacques Chwat
Mr. and Mrs. E. L. Doctorow
Caroline Du Crocq
The Findhorn Gardens
Ludwig Flazen
David Franke
George W. George
Jerzy Grotowski
Valerie Harris
Beverly Karp
Howard Klein and The
  Rockefeller Foundation
Steve and Dede Leiber
The Lindisfarne Association
Porter MacCray
China Machado
Elzbieta Majewska
Louis Malle
Vincent Malle

Gail Merrifield
Charles and Diana Michener
Rena Mirecka
Renata Niemierowska
Panajotis Panajotidis
Joseph Papp
The Polish Lab Theatre
Ewa Prokop
Margaret Ramsay
Keith W. Rouse
Joseph Ruff
Evelyn Sanford
Alan U. Schwartz
Jeri Sopanen
Max Stafford-Clark
William Erwin Thompson
Jeffrey Ullman
Stuart E. Ullman
Robin van Lobensels
Shelley Wanger
Tom Welch
Michael White
Anna Wilga
Krysztof Zdybat

Preface André Gregory, *June, 1981*

Six years ago, when I was still running my theater group, The Manhattan Project, Twyla Tharp choreographed the group and me in a four-and-a-half-minute piece which we performed in concert at Town Hall. The piece was absolutely impossible to do. There was no way that a group of non-dancers could do it. It was incredibly fast, and there must have been hundreds of steps in it. In order to get through it at all, you had to forget yourself, abandon yourself, completely. In rehearsal, Twyla treated us as if we had all trained for years with the American Ballet Theater. "Do this," she'd say, and we would, and she'd laugh, and then, "Do this," and we would, and she'd laugh, and when we reached performance twelve hundred people leapt to their feet and gave us a dozen curtain calls. There were tears of laughter on people's faces. We had danced one of Twyla's most complex creations with absolute precision very, very badly.

For some reason, the experience with Twyla brought to life the White Rabbit in me, and without thinking, in the heat of the moment, like Alice, I followed it down a rabbit hole and gave up my career as a theater director. I embarked on a series of adventures. I went to Asia. I went to North Africa. I stayed up till odd hours of the morning talking to Buddhists and physicists about ancient mysteries. Many of my friends and most of my colleagues thought I was at best ill advised and at worst mad. This went on for about three years, until I reached a moment when for some reason my adventures began to seem to me somehow less frightening, less adventurous. One day, just as I was making plans, without too much enthusiasm, to travel to a Polish mountainside where twenty men and twenty women would come for forty days and forty nights to build an ark and live the life of the ark, I found myself going to see my old friend Wally Shawn, the playwright. I told him that I thought we should drop everything, go to Atlantic City, rent a hotel room for a month, and write a musical together. Wally thought it was a terrible idea.

A year later Wally phoned me and said that this time *he* had an idea for a collaboration. He came over to see me and said that he felt that either I had had a complete nervous breakdown over the last few years, or else a creative block, or a spiritual awakening, or a combination of all three, but whatever it was, when he reached my age (Wally is ten years younger than I am) he didn't want to go through the same thing. And then he proposed that we should sit down together a few times a week and talk and that I should tell him about all the things I had experienced since leaving the theater, and that we should create a fictional piece—a film—based on our talks, and performed by us. I loved the idea, first because there were certain feelings and thoughts that for a long time I had strongly wanted to share with others, and this might be my opportunity to do that, and second because here was a chance for me to return to my old activity of making something for an audience to see, while at the same time surprising myself in the new adventure of being a writer and an actor instead of being a director, and third because it immediately struck me that the most necessary and appropriate piece that one *could* possibly do at this particular moment in history would be a piece about two friends sitting and talking to each other. So Wally and I immediately began to discuss what kind of a work this could be and what might be its themes. And then when Wally left my apartment, I was struck by a peculiar sensation. I had felt all along that the road I'd been traveling in the last few years was sure to end up in some fascinating city. Suddenly now I had the impression that I could see some spires glimmering just ahead.

A few weeks ago I had dinner with Twyla Tharp in her kitchen, and we were talking about the problems of the artist, or for that matter the individual, maturing in our society. Why do we have so few mature artists? Trying to answer this question, we began to speculate that your early years, say your twenties, should be all about learning—learning how to do it, how to say it, learning to master the tools of your craft; having learned the techniques, then your next several years, say your thirties, should be all about telling the world with passion and conviction everything that you think you know about your life and your art. Meanwhile, though, if you have any sense, you'll begin to realize that you just don't know very much—you don't know enough. And so the next many, many years, we agreed, should be all about questions, only questions, and that if you can totally give up your life and your work to questioning, then perhaps somewhere in your midfifties you may find some very small answers to share with others in your work. The problem is that our sociey (including the community of artists) doesn't have much patience with questions and questioning. We want answers, and we want them fast. *My Dinner With André* uses some of the experiences of my six years out of the theater as foundation stones for a work which is made up entirely of questions and which I would like to dedicate to all, artists and otherwise, who are out on the road somewhere wandering, with no destination anywhere in sight, almost forgetting why they ever set out in the first place, yet still unable to turn back, because they honestly believe that the shortest distance between two points just may not be a straight line.

Preface   Wallace Shawn, *June, 1981*

I'd been working as a playwright for ten years. My plays
had been intense, extreme, even maniacal. That was fine,
but now I wanted to do something else, and I didn't know
how. The world of my imagination was becoming a prison
—I knew every inch of the walls, the floor, and the ceiling.
Meanwhile the real world, with its bounteous profusion
of fascinating everyday-ness, was lying resplendent outside
the gates, winking at me, beyond my grasp. I had gener-
ously shown on the stage my interior life as a raging beast,
but my exterior life as a mediocre human being and dilet-
tante of normal intelligence remained unchronicled. And
although my conscious, rational self had cried for expression for years, my unconscious self still kept a brutal
grip on my pen. I knew—I *knew*—that beneath my work's
primeval, hysterical façade there was a calm little writer in
an armchair just waiting to burst forth, but I didn't know
how to reach him; he'd been repressed too savagely for
too long. Meanwhile André Gregory kept asking me to
write a play for him to direct, but I saw nothing in that
project that was likely to help me with my problem. Then
suddenly it occurred to me—My God, what if, instead of a
play, we just did a very simple film, with lots of closeups,
in which I would be talking with André? He would say
absurd things, I would say absurd things, and we would
just talk, as people really do. And instead of just writing it
myself out of my imagination, André and I would really

13

talk for a while, and then my script would be based on our real conversations, and I would use his words and his ideas— It wouldn't just be me! And the piece would say what he wanted it to say, as well as what I wanted it to say. It would be his piece too.

I knew immediately that it would take forever, and it would really require some brains—I'd have to distort us both slightly—our conflicts would have to be sharpened— we'd have to become—well—*characters*. And there would have to be some format, some setting. . . . It would be an enormously elaborate piece of construction. But the great thing about it was that the only commodity I would need to supply would be simple labor—inspired genius was not required! If André agreed to be the hero, then how could it fail? The combination was great, and everything else would follow from that. If André could be persuaded to accept my proposal, my writing problem would be painlessly solved in a pleasant year of easy work.

As I walked to André's apartment, I reflected that, if André was the man I knew him to be, he just wouldn't be able to resist an idea that was dangerous and funny at the same time. As it turned out, I was absolutely right. We sat in his living room, and he immediately said yes. All I had to do after that was just lean back, relax, and sharpen a few pencils.

MY DINNER WITH ANDRÉ

WALLY *is trudging through the streets of New York.*

WALLY (*voice-over*): The life of a playwright is tough. It's not easy, as some people seem to think. You work hard writing plays, and nobody puts them on. You take up other lines of work to try to make a living—acting, in my case—and people don't hire you. So you spend your days crossing the city back and forth doing the errands of your trade. Today wasn't any easier than any other day. I'd had to be up by ten to make some important phone calls, then I'd gone to the stationery store to buy envelopes, and then to the xerox shop. There were dozens of things to do. By five o'clock I'd finally made it to the post office and mailed off several copies of my plays, meanwhile checking constantly with my answering service to see if my agent had called with any acting work. In the morning, the mailbox had been stuffed with bills. What was I supposed to do? How was I supposed to pay them? After all, I was doing my best. (*He keeps trudging.*) I've lived in this city all my life. I grew up on the Upper East Side, and when I was ten years old I was rich, I was an aristocrat, riding around in taxis, surrounded by comfort, and all I thought about was art and music. Now I'm thirty-six, and all I think about is money. (*He goes into the subway.*) It was now seven o'clock, and I would have liked nothing better than to go home and have my girlfriend, Debby, cook me a nice delicious dinner. But for the last several years our financial circumstances have forced her to work three nights a week as a waitress—after all, playwriting doesn't pay for the salt, much less the bread on the table, and we had to have *some* money coming in—so I was on my own. But the worst thing of all was that I had been trapped by an odd series of events into agreeing to have dinner with a man I'd been avoiding literally for years, and I was looking forward to the evening with a feeling of absolute dread. His name was André Gregory. At one time, he'd been not only a close friend of mine, but my most valued theatrical colleague. In fact, he was the man who had first discovered me and put one of my plays on the professional stage. When I had known André, he'd been at the height of his career as a theater director. The work he did with his company, The Manhattan Project—their productions of *Alice in Wonderland, Endgame, The Seagull*—had been acclaimed as brilliant and extraordinary throughout the world. (WALLY *is walking down another street.*) But then, after doing my play, *Our Late Night,* something had happened to André. No one knew quite what. He had dropped out of the theater. For months at a time his family seemed only to know that he was traveling by himself in odd parts of the world—which was very surprising, because André was known to be crazy about his wife and children and never used to like to leave home. You would occasionally hear that he'd been seen following around at the heels of some Buddhist monk or else that someone had seen him at a party, and he'd been telling people that he'd talked with trees or something like that. It was obvious that something terrible had happened to André, and the whole idea of meeting him made me very nervous. I mean, I really wasn't up for this sort of thing. I had problems of my own. I couldn't help André—was I supposed to be a doctor, or what?

WALLY *enters a lovely-looking restaurant on a nice-looking street. He leaves his coat in the cloakroom*

*and is directed to the bar, where he stands for a
while, waiting and looking around, while his voice-
over continues.*

WALLY (*voice-over*): When I'd called André, and he'd suggested that we meet at this expensive restaurant, I'd
been rather surprised, because André's tastes used to
be very ascetic, even though everybody knows that
he's got some money hidden away somewhere—I
mean, how the hell else could he have been flying
off to Asia or wherever he went and still have been
supporting his family? (WALLY *continues to look
around.*) The reason I was meeting André in the first
place was that an acquaintance of mine, George
Grassfield, had called me up a couple of days ago and
just insisted that I had to see him. Apparently
George had been out walking his dog in some odd
section of town when he had suddenly come upon a
solitary man leaning against a crumbling building,
sobbing uncontrollably. Well, George was about
to walk by rapidly, as one does in New York, when
he suddenly realized that the man was André. So
George had gone up to him and put his arm around
him. And then they'd gone someplace nearby to have
a cup of coffee, and André had explained to him that
he'd been watching the Ingmar Bergman movie *Au-
tumn Sonata* about twenty-five blocks away, and he'd
been seized by a fit of ungovernable crying when the
character played by Ingrid Bergman had said, "I
could always live in my art, but never in my life."

WALLY *suddenly sees* ANDRÉ *approaching.*

ANDRÉ: My God—Wally!

WALLY: Hi, André.

ANDRÉ *and* WALLY *meet and hug.*

(*Voice-over*) I remember, when I first started working with André's company, I couldn't get over the way the actors would *hug* when they greeted people. "Now I'm really in the theater," I thought.

WALLY *and* ANDRÉ *stand by the bar.*

(*To* ANDRÉ) You look terrific.

ANDRÉ (*warmly*): Well, thank you. I *feel* terrible.

They both laugh loudly and continue talking.

WALLY (*voice-over*): I was feeling incredibly nervous. I wasn't sure I could stick through an entire meal with him. He looked crazy to me. (*Cut to* ANDRÉ's *face.*) He was talking about Jerzy Grotowski, the great Polish theater director—a close friend of his, and in a way his guru. After becoming the most respected experimental theater director in the world, Grotowski had dropped out of the theater, just a couple of years before André did. Grotowski had once been a rather fat man, who had worn black suits and a tie.

A WAITER *approaches. He is in his seventies. His face shows that he has seen and experienced the suffering of the world. He leads* ANDRÉ *and* WALLY *to a table.*

WALLY (*voice-over*): Eventually I thought to myself that the only way to make this evening bearable would be to find out as much as I could about the person I happened to be with. I always enjoy finding out about people. It always relaxes me. In fact, my secret profession, in a way—secret from everyone but me—is that I'm a private investigator, a detective. I always want to ask questions. (ANDRÉ *and* WALLY *look at menus.*) In fact, if someone tells me their best friend has just died, it takes a terrific effort of will on my part not to immediately say, "Hey! Wow! Your friend died? Well, how do you feel? What was it like?" Once, when I was seventeen years old, I was standing with a favorite teacher of mine when we happened to observe a group of people caught in a painful but, to me, comical situation. As I was laughing cheerfully at their plight, my teacher surprised me by saying, "Wally, other people were not put on the earth just to serve as objects for your amusement." Well, I'm sure he was right, but a person can't help his own nature.

WALLY *looks up from his menu.*

(*To* ANDRÉ) By the way, is he still thin?

ANDRÉ: What?

WALLY: Grotowski—is he still thin?

ANDRÉ: Oh, absolutely.

They order.

WALLY (*voice-over*):
So we talked for a while about my writing and my acting and about my girlfriend, Debby, and we talked

about his wife, Chiquita, and his two children, Nicolas and Marina. Finally I got around to asking him
what he'd been up to in the last few years. He
seemed a little reluctant to go into it, but that made
me all the more anxious to know the story. I was sure
I would feel very relaxed with him if only he'd tell
me his story. So I just kept asking, and finally he
started to answer.

Close-up on ANDRÉ's *face, talking. As* WALLY's *voice-
over ends,* ANDRÉ's *voice slowly fades up.*

ANDRÉ: So this was about five years ago, and Grotowski
and I were walking along Fifth Avenue, and we were
talking, and you see, he'd invited me to come and
teach that summer in Poland—you know, teach a
workshop to actors and directors or whatever. And I
had told him that I didn't want to come, because,
really, I had nothing left to teach. I had nothing left
to say. I didn't know anything. I couldn't teach anything. Exercises meant nothing to me anymore.
Working on scenes from plays seemed ridiculous. I
didn't know what to do. I mean, I just couldn't do it.
And so he said to me, "Why don't you tell me anything you would like to have if you did a workshop
for me, no matter how outrageous, and maybe I can
give it to you." So I said, kind of jokingly, although
in retrospect it makes great sense, I said, "If you
could give me forty Jewish women who speak neither
English nor French, either women who have been in
the theater for a long time and want to leave it but
don't know why, or young women who love the theater but have never seen a theater they could love, and
if these women could play the trumpet or the harp,

and if I could work in a forest, I'd come." And we both laughed a lot. And then a week later or two weeks later he called me from Poland. And he said, "Well, you know, forty Jewish women are a little hard to find," but he said, "I do have forty women. They all fit pretty much the definition." And he said, "I also have some very interesting men, but you don't have to work with them. These are all people who have in common the fact that they're questioning the theater. They don't all play the trumpet or the harp, but they all play a musical instrument. And none of them speak English." And he'd found me a forest, Wally, and the only inhabitants of the forest were some wild boar and a hermit. So that was an offer I couldn't refuse.

WALLY: Huh.

ANDRÉ: I had to go.

WALLY: Gosh.

ANDRÉ: So I went to Poland, and I had this wonderful group of young men and women. And you know, the forest he found us was absolutely magical, Wally, and you know, it was a huge forest—I mean, the trees were so large that four or five people linking their arms couldn't get their arms around the trees. And so we were camped out beside the ruins of a tiny little castle, and we would eat around this great stone slab that served as a sort of a table, and our schedule was that we would usually start work around sunset, and then we'd generally work until six or seven in the morning, and then, because the Poles loved to sing and dance, we'd generally sing and dance till about ten or eleven in the morning, and then we'd have our food, which was generally bread, jam, cheese, and tea, and then we'd sleep from about noon to sunset. And now technically, of course, technically, the situation was a very interesting one, because if you find yourself in a forest with a group of forty people who don't speak your language, then all your moorings are gone.

WALLY: Right.

ANDRÉ: To do scenes, or improvisations, or exercises in this kind of forest is ridiculous. And then, the question is, if you're not a tourist, if you can't be there as a tourist, if you can't be there in a certain sense as a maker of art or creator of art, what to do.

WALLY: Uh-huh.

ANDRÉ: What do you do? What do you do that has any kind of meaning or importance?

WALLY: Yes.

ANDRÉ: Well you see, this experience in Poland was the first of many experiences that I led—or you can call them workshops, by analogy with the old workshops I used to teach when I was teaching acting in New York—but these new workshops were very different, because the basis of *these* workshops is just to create some terrible hole that we would all drop into. And that's usually quite frightening, because we don't know where we will be at the next moment.

WALLY: What do you mean, exactly?

ANDRÉ: Well, what we do is just sit there and wait for someone to have an impulse to do something. Now, in a way that's something like a theatrical improvisation.

WALLY: Yes.

ANDRÉ: I mean, you know, if you were a director working on a play by Chekhov, you might have the actors playing the mother, the son, and the uncle all sit in a room and do a made-up scene that isn't in the play. For example, you would say to them, "All right, let's say that it's a rainy Sunday afternoon on Sorin's estate, and you're all trapped in the drawing room together," and everyone would improvise, saying and doing what their characters might say and do in that circumstance.

WALLY: Uh-huh.

ANDRÉ: Except that in the improvisations in these workshops, the theme is oneself.

WALLY: Right.

ANDRÉ: So you follow the same law of improvisation, which is that you do whatever your impulse—as the character—tells you to do, but in this case *you're* the character, so you have no imaginary situation to hide behind, and you have no other person to hide behind. What you're doing, in fact, is asking those questions that Stanislavski said that the actor should constantly ask himself as a character—Who am I? Why am I here? Where do I come from? and Where am I going?—but instead of applying them to a role, you apply them to yourself. So, in other words, in these workshops, a group of people come together, and I would go on the assumption that something had brought us together—

WALLY: Uh-huh.

ANDRÉ: —and that the theme or the plot was made up of who we all were together, and that the question then was how to bring to action this theme—

WALLY: Yes.

ANDRÉ: —to find the theme through action. And that the action was created by impulse, by somebody having an impulse. In a way it's going right back to child-hood, where simply a group of children enter a room or are brought into a room, without toys, and they begin to play. Grown-ups were learning how to play again.

WALLY: Yes. Right. So you would all sit together some-where, and you would play in some way—but what would you actually do?

ANDRÉ: Well, I can give you a good example. You see, we worked for a week in the city before we went to our forest, and of course Grotowski was there in the city too, and, you see, one of the things I asked Grotowski was that I be kept as far away from him as possible so

I couldn't be influenced by him in any way, because his whole group was leading workshops. But I did hear that every night they conducted something called a beehive. And I loved the sound of this beehive, and a night or two before we were supposed to go to the country I grabbed him by the collar, and I said, "Listen, this beehive thing, you know, I'd kind of like to participate in one, just instinctively I feel it would be something interesting." And he said, "Well, certainly, and in fact, why don't you, with your group, *lead* a beehive instead of participating in one?" And I got very nervous, you know, and I said, "Well, what *is* a beehive?" And he said, "Well, a beehive is, at eight o'clock a hundred strangers come into a room." And I said, "Yes?" And he said, "Yes, and then whatever happens is a beehive."

WALLY: Ha ha!

ANDRÉ: And I said, "Yes, but what am I supposed to do?" He said, "That's up to you." And I said, "No—I really don't want to do this." (*He laughs.*) "I'll just participate." And he said, "No, no, you lead the beehive." And I was really terrified, Wally, because in a way I felt on stage.

WALLY: Right.

ANDRÉ: And also, suddenly I felt I was going to be judged by the great Pole. But I did it. And what I remember of it—well, it is a good example.

WALLY: God—tell me about it.

ANDRÉ: Now I have a tape of this song—I can play it for you some day, it's just unbelievably beautiful—I mean, talk about, you know, what amateurs can create. Well, one of the young women in our group knew a few fragments of one of the *most* beautiful songs of St. Francis. It's a song in which you thank God for your eyes, you thank God for your heart, you thank God for your friends, you thank God for your life, and it's—it repeats itself over and over again. And that became our theme song, and I must play this thing some day, because you just can't *believe* that a group of people who don't know how to sing could create something so beautiful, but it was because we were really in great harmony. But I decided that when the people arrived for the beehive that our group would already be there singing this song, and that we would simply sing it and sing it and sing it until something happened.

WALLY: Uh-huh.

ANDRÉ: Because it was a very beautiful song. And one person wanted to bring her very large teddy bear, because she felt a little afraid of this event, and this teddy bear had been something that as a little child she had loved, and somebody wanted to bring a sheet. Somebody else wanted to bring a large bowl of water in case people got hot and thirsty. And somebody suggested that we have candles and that there be no artificial light, but candlelight.

WALLY: Mm-hmm—

ANDRÉ: So there was nothing but this song, a teddy bear,

water, a sheet, and candles. Now, of course this was very similar, Wally, to the theater, because I remember, before this thing began, feeling sort of like an old actor who was about to go on stage but didn't really know his lines yet. And all the critics were going to be there. I was terrified. And I remember watching people preparing for this evening, and of course there was no makeup, there were no costumes, but it was exactly the way people prepare for a performance. You know, people sort of taking off their jewelry and their watches and stowing them away and making sure it's all secure. And then slowly people arrived, the way they would arrive at the theater, in ones and twos and tens and fifteens and what have you, and we were just sitting, and we were singing this very beautiful song, and people started to sit with us and started to *learn* the song.

WALLY: Uh-huh.

ANDRÉ: Even though nothing in what we did led them to do it. In other words, it could have gone in any other direction—

WALLY: Uh-huh.

ANDRÉ: —you see. And after a while they were, whatever it was, a hundred and something people who were all singing this very beautiful song together, and we sang it over and over again. Now there is, of course, as in any improvisation or a performance, an instinct for when it's going to get boring.

WALLY: Ha ha.

ANDRÉ: So, at a certain point, but I think it may have taken an hour to get there, or an hour and a half, I suddenly *grabbed* this teddy bear and *threw* it into the air—

WALLY: Heh heh heh—

ANDRÉ: —at which a hundred and forty or thirty or whatever people suddenly *exploded*, you know, it was like a Jackson Pollock painting in—suddenly human beings *exploded* from this tight little circle that was singing this song, and before I knew it, there were two circles, dancing, you know, one dancing clockwise, the other dancing counterclockwise, with rhythm mostly from the waist down, in other words like an American Indian dance, with a kind of thumping, persistent rhythm.

WALLY: Uh-huh.

ANDRÉ: Now in a way you can see where the line between this, or a religious ceremony, or a primitive tribal ritual, and something like Hitler's Nuremburg rallies was really a very thin line, because of course all of these things depend on repetition, because we're talking in a sense about group trance, and for any kind of trance, of course, rhythm is essential.

WALLY: Right . . . Yes . . .

ANDRÉ: But anyway, there were these two huge circles going in different directions around each other with this thumping going on, and in the center of it—now, Grotowski had come to be a participant in this thing,

and you see, I don't know how this happened, because it happened completely spontaneously—

WALLY: Yes.

ANDRÉ: —and fast—but in the center of this thing were
Grotowski and I sitting opposite each other, and we
threw the teddy bear back and forth.

WALLY: Uh-huh—

ANDRÉ: You know, on one level you could say this is childish. And I gave the teddy bear suck, suddenly, at my
breast, while the—*vomp vomp vomp*—chanting was
going on—

WALLY: Uh-huh.

ANDRÉ: —and then I threw the teddy bear to him, and he
gave it suck at his breast. Then the teddy bear went
up into the air and then again an *explosion* of form
into—something else—

WALLY: Uh-huh—

ANDRÉ: —and these, you see—what was it like? This is the
—you know, there's something—like a kaleidoscope,
like a human kaleidoscope.

WALLY: Yes. Yes.

ANDRÉ: The evening was made up of shiftings of the kaleidoscope. Now, the only things that I remember
other than constantly trying to guide this thing,

which was always either involved with movement, rhythm, repetition, or song—

WALLY: Right—

ANDRÉ: —or chanting—

WALLY: Right—

ANDRÉ: —because two people in my group brought musical instruments, a flute and a drum, which of course are sacred instruments—was that *sometimes* the room would break up into six or seven different things going on at once.

WALLY: Mm-hmm.

ANDRÉ: Six or seven different improvisations, all of which seemed to be in some way related to each other—it was like a magnificent cobweb. At one point—this was very interesting—I noticed that Grotowski was the center of one group huddled around a bunch of candles that they'd gotten together, and like a little child fascinated by fire—because in this moment the room was really quite quiet—

WALLY: Uh-huh.

ANDRÉ: —there was a group chanting in one corner, a group doing something else in another corner—and I felt in that moment I could go with my own impulse, you know, and follow *my* impulse instead of trying to be aware of the whole thing—I saw that Grotowski had his hand right in the flame and was holding it there, and I approached this group, and I wondered if I could do it. And I put my left hand in the flame, and I could hold it there as long as I liked, and there was no burn. And no pain. But when I put my *right* hand in the flame, I couldn't hold it there for a second. So Grotowski said, "If it burns, change some little thing in yourself," and I tried to do that, but it didn't work. And then I remember a very, very beautiful procession with the sheet, and with somebody being carried below the sheet—the sheet was like some great biblical canopy—and with the entire group weaving around the room, chanting. And then I remember a moment when people were dancing, and I was dancing with a girl, and suddenly our hands were vibrating near each other, like this, vibrating, vibrating, and then we went down to our knees, and suddenly I was sobbing in her arms, and she was sort of cradling me in her arms, and then she started to cry too, and then we just hugged each other for a moment, and then we joined the dance again. And then at a certain point, hours later, we returned to the singing of the song of St. Francis, and I think I lost my nerve there, because I probably should have gone longer. On the other hand, my point of view is different from the Poles'. The Poles are, you know, like Marines—they would have gone on all night!

WALLY: Ha ha—

ANDRÉ: My impulse is that if the show's been good—

WALLY: Right—

ANDRÉ: —get out and leave them laughing.

WALLY: Right.

ANDRÉ: So I think that this thing lasted four or five hours instead of eight or ten. So after we'd been singing the song for another fifteen or twenty minutes or I don't know what, I gathered two of the people in my group, and we went to the door, and I gestured to the people that they could leave, that it was over. And the farewell took two hours, at least, because nobody left until they had a true impulse to leave. You see, also we're talking about trying to find the truthful impulse, to not do what you should do or ought to do or what is expected of you, but trying to find what it is that you really want to do or need to do or have to do. So the singing went on, and people left as they wanted to leave, and what was really quite amazing was that each person said farewell to the three of us, and especially to me, but in no single case, really, was the farewell the same—

WALLY: Uh-huh—

ANDRÉ: —so that one person would just shake me by the hand and walk out, another person might—I still have a very beautiful cross that somebody simply took from around their neck—a total stranger that I never saw again, and I can't even remember who it was— and put around *my* neck. One person jumped up on my back and rode me around the room like a horse.

WALLY: Ha ha ha—

ANDRÉ: While people sang. And then, again, when it was over, it was like the theater after a performance. Everyone put on their earrings and their wristwatches

and went off to the railroad station to drink a lot of beer and have a good dinner. And there was one girl who wasn't in our group but who just wouldn't leave, and we took her along with us.

WALLY: Huh. Incredible.

The WAITER *brings the first course.*

God. Well, tell me about some of the other work that you did with your group. . . .

ANDRÉ: Well, it's very hard to describe what went on in Poland, Wally. I remember once when we were still in the city, the people in the group somehow got me to understand the idea that they really wanted me to do at least *something* with them that was like the sort of work I used to do in New York. So we did this kind of ordinary, banal improvisation where everybody was supposed to be on a plane, and they've just learned from the pilot that something was wrong with the motor. But what was unusual about this improvisation was that two people who participated in it fell in love—they've in fact married.

WALLY: Ha ha ha ha!

ANDRÉ: And when we went to—out of the fear of being on this plane, they fell in love, thinking they were going to die any moment—and when we went to the forest, these two disappeared, because they understood the experiment so well that they realized that to go off with each other in the forest was much more important than doing any kind of experiment that the group could do as a whole.

WALLY: Uh-huh—

ANDRÉ: So about halfway through the week we stumbled into a clearing in the forest, and the two of them were fast asleep in each other's arms—it was around dawn. And we put flowers on them so that they'd know we'd been there, and we crept away.

WALLY: Ha ha ha—

ANDRÉ: And on the last day of our stay in the forest these two showed up, and they shook my hands, and they thanked me very much for the wonderful work that they'd been able to do, you see.

WALLY: Ha ha.

ANDRÉ: So they understood what it was about. I mean, that of course poses the question of what was it about. But it was something to do with living. (*Pause.*) And then on the final day in the forest the whole group did something so wonderful for me, Wally. They arranged a christening—a baptism—for me. And they filled the castle with flowers. And it was just a miracle of light, because they had set up literally hundreds of candles and torches. I mean, no church could have looked more beautiful. And there was a simple ceremony, and one of them played the role of my godfather and one of them played the role of my godmother, and I was given a new name. They called me Yendrush. And you know, some of them took it completely seriously, and some of them found it funny. But I really felt that I had a new name. And then we had an enormous feast, with blueberries

picked from the fields, and chocolates that someone had gone a great distance to buy, and raspberry soup, and rabbit stew. And then we sang Polish songs and Greek songs and every kind of song, and everyone danced for the rest of the night.

He takes a photograph from his wallet and shows it to WALLY. *Close-up of picture.*

You see—that was me in the forest. That was what I felt like. See, that's the state I was in.

WALLY: God—who's this?

WALLY *holds a picture of* ANDRÉ *and an intense young woman with long braids.*

ANDRÉ *(laughs)*: That was—er—that was a young woman who was nicknamed with an Indian name.

WALLY: I wonder why. (*They both laugh.*) That's incredible. Incredible.

ANDRÉ: But she's Polish. She now—she now works in a Russian restaurant in London.

WALLY: Ha ha— (*Pause.*) Well—André— Gosh. Yes, I remember George telling me that he'd met you right around then, and he said you looked like you'd come back from a war or something.

ANDRÉ: Yes, I remember meeting him. He asked me a lot of friendly questions. I think I called you up too that summer, didn't I?

WALLY: Well, I think I was out of town.

ANDRÉ: Yeah, well most people I met thought there was something wrong with me. They didn't say that, but I could tell that that was what they thought. But you see, what *I* think I experienced was for the first time in my life to know what it means to be truly alive.

WALLY: Mm-hmm.

ANDRÉ: Now, that's very frightening, because with that comes an immediate awareness of death—

WALLY: Mm-hmm.

ANDRÉ: —because they go hand in hand. The kind of impulse that led to Walt Whitman—that led to *Leaves of Grass*, you know, that feeling of being connected with everything, means to also be connected with death. And that's pretty scary. But I really felt as if I were *floating* above the ground, not walking. And you know, I could do things like go out to the highway and watch the lights go from red to green and think, How wonderful. It was a feeling of recognising everything, of being able to be aware of the reality and the specialness of even the most ordinary things. And that feeling lasted for quite a while, and then gradually it faded. And then one day in the early fall I was out in the country, walking in a field, and I suddenly heard a voice say, "*Little Prince.*" Now *The Little Prince*, of course, was a book that I had always thought of as disgusting, childish treacle, but still, I thought, Well, if a voice comes to me in a field—this was the first voice I had ever heard—maybe I should go and read the book. Now that same morning I had gotten a letter from one of the women who had been in my group in Poland. And in her letter she had said, "You have dominated me." She spoke, you know, very awkward English. And so she'd gone to the dictionary, and she'd crossed out the word "dominated" and written, "No, the correct word is 'tamed.' " And then when I went into town and bought the book and started to read it, I saw that "taming" was the most important word in the whole book. And by the end of the book I was in tears, I was so moved by the story. And I went to try to write an answer to the letter, because she'd sent me a very long letter, but I just couldn't find the right words. So finally I took my hand, put it on a piece of paper and outlined it with a pen and put in the center something like "Your heart is in my hand"—something like that. And then I went over to my brother's house to swim, because he lives nearby in the country and he has a pool, and he wasn't there. And I went into his library, and he had bought at an auction the collected issues of *Minotaur*—you know, the surrealist magazine—it was a great, great surrealist magazine of the twenties and thirties that had all kinds of people like Dali and so on—and I had never—because I consider myself a bit of a surrealist—I had never ever seen a copy of *Minotaur*. And here they were, bound, year after year. So, at random, I picked one out, and I opened it, and there was a full-page reproduction of the letter "A" from Tenniel's *Alice in Wonderland*. And I thought, That's— Well, you know, it's been a day of coincidences, but that's not unusual, that the surrealists would have been interested in *Alice* and I did a play of *Alice*. So I opened to another page, and there were four handprints. One was André Breton, another was André Derain, the third was André—I've got it written down somewhere, it's not Malraux, it's like—someone—another of the surrealists—all A's— and the fourth was Antoine de Saint-Exupéry, who wrote *The Little Prince*. And they'd given these handprints to some kind of an expert without saying whose hands they belonged to, and under Saint-Exupéry it said he was an artist with very powerful eyes who was a tamer of wild animals. So I thought, This is incredible, you know. And I looked back to see when this issue came out, and it came out on the newsstands May 12, 1934, and I was born during the day of May 11, 1934.

WALLY: Huh. My goodness—

The WAITER *brings the wine.*

ANDRÉ: So that was what started me with Saint-Exupéry and *The Little Prince*.

WALLY: Gosh—

ANDRÉ: Now of course today I think there's a very fascistic thing under *The Little Prince*. I think there's a kind of SS totalitarian sentimentality in there somewhere. There's something—you know, that love of—that masculine love of a certain kind of oily muscle—you know what I mean?

WALLY: Mm-hmm.

ANDRÉ: I can't quite put my finger on it, but—I can just imagine a beautiful SS man loving *The Little Prince*.

André Gregory. (Photo: Diana Michener)

Wallace Shawn. *(Photo: Keith Rouse)*

Jean Lenauer as the waiter.

(Photo: *Diana Michener*)

André Gregory. *(Photo: Diana Michener)*

Wallace Shawn and André Gregory. *(Photo: Diana Michener)*

(Photo: Diana Michener)

Wallace Shawn.

(Photo: Diana Michener)

Wallace Shawn and André Gregory. *(Photo: Diana Michener)*

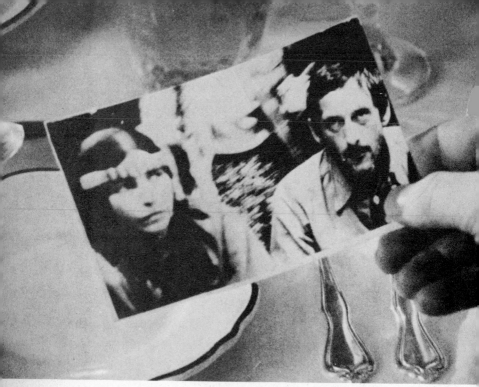

André in the Polish forest.

WALLY: Uh-huh.

ANDRÉ: I don't know why, but there's something wrong with it—it stinks.

WALLY: Yes. (*Pause.*) Didn't George once tell me that you were going to do a play based on *The Little Prince?*

ANDRÉ: Well, what happened, Wally, was that that fall I was in New York, and I met this young Japanese Buddhist priest named Kozan, and I thought he was Puck from the *Midsummer Night's Dream*, Wally— you know, he had this beautiful delicate smile—I thought he was the Little Prince. And so naturally I decided to go to the Sahara desert to work on *The Little Prince* with two actors and this Japanese priest.

WALLY: You did?

ANDRÉ: And I mean, I was still in a pretty peculiar state at that time, Wally—you know, I would look in the rear-view mirror of my car, and I would see little birds flying out of my mouth. And I remember always being exhausted in that period—I always felt weak— and I really didn't know what was going on with me— I would just sit out there alone in the country for days and really do nothing except write a little bit in my diary, and I was always thinking about death.

WALLY: But you went to the Sahara—

ANDRÉ: Yes, we went off into the desert, and we rode through the desert on camels, and we rode and rode, and then at night we would walk out under that enormous sky and look at the stars, and I just kept thinking about the same things I was thinking about at home—particularly about Chiquita—in fact I thought about just about nothing but my marriage. And I remember one incredibly dark night being at an oasis where there were palm trees moving in the wind, and hearing Kozan singing somewhere far away in a beautiful bass voice, and following his voice along the sand. You know, I thought he had something to teach me, Wally. And sometimes I would meditate with him. And then sometimes I would go off and meditate by myself, and I would see images of Chiquita. Once I actually saw her growing old and her hair turning gray in front of my eyes. And you know, I would just wail and yell my lungs out, out there on those dunes. Anyway, the desert was pretty horrible, pretty cold. We were searching for something, but we couldn't tell if we were finding anything. Once Kozan and I were sitting out on a dune, and we just ate sand. We weren't trying to be funny. I started, and he started, and we just ate sand, and threw up. That was—that was how desperate we were. In other words, we didn't know why we were there. We didn't know what we were looking for. The whole thing seemed completely absurd, arid, empty, and it was like a last chance or something.

WALLY: Uh-huh. Right. So what happened then?

ANDRÉ: Well, in those days I went completely on impulse, so on impulse I brought Kozan back to stay with us in New York after we got back from the Sahara, and he stayed for six months. And he really sort of took over the whole family, in a way.

WALLY: What do you mean?

ANDRÉ: Well, there was certainly a center missing in the house at the time. There certainly wasn't a father, because I was always thinking about going off to Tibet or doing God knows what. And so he taught the whole family to meditate, and he told them all about Asia and the East and his monastery and everything. And he really captivated everyone with an incredible bag of tricks. You know, he could do anything—anything. There was nothing he couldn't do. You know, if he suddenly wanted to—you know, the Christmas tree didn't have decorations—he would make them, out of nowhere. And I mean, he had literally developed himself, Wally, so that he could push on his fingers and rise off—out of his chair. In other words, he could—literally—go like this. Go up, uh, on two fingers—go into like a head stand, and just hold himself up with two fingers. And he would constantly be doing these things, you know—and he knew about everything. I mean, he was a great doctor. In other words—if you were tense, you know—say Chiquita would suddenly get a little tension in her neck—well, he would immediately have her on the floor, and he'd be walking up and down her back and doing unbelievable massages, you know. And of course the children found him amazing. I mean, Nicolas would do a chin-up, and then Kozan would do a thousand! I mean, he had an incredible way with children. You know, we would visit friends who had children, and immediately he was playing with those children in a way that, you know, we just can't do. Those children just—*giggles, giggles, giggles*, you know, about what this Japanese monk was doing in these holy robes. I mean, he was an acrobat, a magician, a ventriloquist—everything. And the amazing thing was that I don't think he had any interest in children what-

soever. None at all. I don't think he liked them.
When he lived with us—I mean, in the first week
really the kids were just googly-eyed, but then Chiquita and I could be out a couple of weeks later, and
Marina could have a fever of a hundred and four or
flu or something like that, and he wouldn't even go in
and say hello to her.

WALLY: Oh.

ANDRÉ: And around Christmastime we were out in the
country a lot, and I used to go out and walk for hours
on the golf course out there—by that time it was
snowing, so the golf course was covered with snow—
and I just was feeling absolutely lost, just absolutely
lost and angry and confused. And Kozan was taking
over more and more. You know, he was telling us
what to have for dinner, and of course his own habits
had completely changed. You know, he started wearing these Gucci leather shoes under his white monk's
robes, and he was eating *huge* amounts of food. I
mean, he ate twice as much as Nicolas ate. This tiny
little Buddhist, who when I first met him, you know,
was eating a little bowl of milk, hot milk with rice,
was now eating huge *beefs*—and it was very strange—
and we had tried to work together, but really our
work had just consisted of my trying to learn to do
these incredibly painful prostrations that they do in
the monastery, so we really hadn't been working very
much. But anyway, we were all out in the country,
and we went to Christmas mass together, and he was
all dressed up in his Buddhist finery, and it was, you
know, one of those awful dreary Catholic churches on
Long Island where the priest talks about Commu-

nism and birth control. And as I was sitting there in mass, I was wondering, What in the world is going on? Here I am, a grown man, and there's this strange person living in our house, and I'm not working—you know, I mean, all I was doing was scribbling a little poetry in my diary—and I can't get a job teaching anymore, and I don't know what I want to do—and all of a sudden a huge creature appeared, looking at the congregation, and it was about, I'd say, six foot eight, something like that, and it was half bull and half man, and its skin was blue, and it had violets growing out of its eyelids and poppies growing out of its toenails. And it stood there for the whole mass. I mean, there was nothing that I could do that would make it disappear. You know, I thought, oh—you know, I thought, well, I'm just seeing this because I'm bored. You know, close my—I mean, I could not make that creature go away.

WALLY: Incredible.

ANDRÉ: Okay. Now, I didn't talk with people about it, because they'd think I was weird, but I felt that this creature had come to me to somehow comfort me. In other words, somehow he was appearing to say, Well, you may feel low and you may not be able to create a play right now, but look at what can come to you on Christmas Eve. Hang on, old friend. I may seem weird to you, but on those weird voyages, you know, weird creatures show up. It's part of the journey. You're okay. Hang in there.

WALLY: God—incredible— (*Long pause.*) By the way, did you ever see that play *The Violets Are Blue?*

ANDRÉ: No.

WALLY: Oh, well when you mentioned the violets it re-
minded me of that. (*Pause.*) It was about—er—people
being strangled on a submarine.

ANDRÉ: Uh-huh.

Silence. Close-up of WALLY's *face perspiring.*

WALLY: Well, so that was Christmas. What happened
after that?

ANDRÉ: Do you really want to hear about all this?

WALLY: Yes.

ANDRÉ: Well, after that, I began to think about going to
India, and Kozan suddenly left one day, and a lot of
strange things started to happen. I was experiencing a
lot of synchronicity—

WALLY: A lot of—

ANDRÉ: Well, you know, as I understand it, Wally, I think
it's possible that in certain periods of your life the
unconscious can have an enormous amount of power,
so that it can actually make manifest what you need
at that time. It can simply give you signs, make people appear, give you the feeling that you're—that
there are so many coincidences that you must be on
the right path. In fact, you could be on the wrong
path, but I got very hot just before I went to India,
and I *was* in a very strange state, and I was very ner-

vous about going to India, and maybe I was at my
most desperate then, but a lot of very strange things
did start to happen. Now, for example, I had developed—I had got this idea which I thought was—it was
very appealing to me at the time—which was that I
would have a flag, a large flag, and that, wherever I
worked, this flag would fly. Or if we were outside, say,
with a group, that the flag could be the thing we lay
on at night, and that somehow between lying on this
flag, working with this flag, this flag flying above us,
the flag would pick up vibrations of a kind and would
become somehow something that I could again bring
back from the journey.

WALLY: Mm-hmm.

ANDRÉ: That I not only needed it as a talisman, that I
needed somehow to bring it back. Anyway, one day
right around that period I was talking to a woman I
know about the nineteen-sixties, and to illustrate a
point I got down from my bookshelf a book of photographs of the sixties that I hadn't looked at in ten
years. And the woman said, "My God, that's one
of my best friends who took those pictures. He's
now a flagmaker." Well, that was incredible, and so
naturally I then went down to meet her friend the
flagmaker, and there was this very straightforward-
looking guy—very sweet, you know, really healthy-
looking and everything, nice, big, blond—and he had
a beautiful clean loft down in the Village with lovely
happy flags, and I was all into *The Little Prince*,
and I talked to him about *The Little Prince* and
these adventures and everything like that and how I
needed this flag and what the flag should be. And he

seemed to really connect with it, and he said, "I understand. Come back in a couple of weeks, and I'll have a design for you." So I came back, and he showed me a design that I thought was very odd, because I had not—I had expected something gentle and lyrical. And there was something about this that was so powerful it was almost overwhelming. And it did include the Tibetan swastika.

WALLY: He put a swastika in your flag?

ANDRÉ: Oh, it was the Tibetan swastika, not the Nazi swastika, it's not the same; it was one of the most ancient Tibetan symbols. And there was the purple of the church, and it was just strange, but very intriguing. And I said, "Well, it's not what I expected, but it's very powerful. Can you show me the kind of material you'd put into it?" And he said, "Oh, sure," you know, and he took me to another part of the loft. And now really, Wally, in this loft all there were were the flags on the wall and two tables. And on one table was the design, and on the other table was the material. So we went and looked at the material, and he showed me how the colors would go against each other, and I said, "Could I see this against the design?" and he said, "Oh, sure," and we went back to the table, and the design was gone. We never found it. We searched the entire loft top to bottom and never found the design. It just disappeared.

WALLY: Gosh.

ANDRÉ: But then my *idea* with this flag was that before I left—before I left for India I wanted several people who were very close to me to have this flag in their rooms for the night to sleep with it. And in the morning to sew something into the flag. So Chiquita threw this party for me as a—before I was leaving for India— and I picked up the flag, and I took it in to Marina because I thought Marina could sleep with it that night. And I said, "Look at this. What do you think of this?" And she said, "What is that? That's awful." I said, "It's a flag." And she said, "I don't like it." And I said, "Oh, well, I just really wanted you to kind of spend the night with it, you know." But she really thought the flag was awful. So I put it back in the bedroom. The apartment was filled with guests by this point, and at one point Chiquita said, "The flag, the flag, where's the flag?" And I said, "Oh, yeah, the flag." And I go and get the flag, and I open the flag out, and Chiquita goes absolutely white and runs out of the room and vomits. And the party just comes to a halt and breaks up. So next I called a very good friend of mine, and I didn't tell her anything about any of this, and I said, "About this flag, what I'd like you to do is to spend the night with it." And she said, "Oh, yeah, what a lovely idea," you know. And the next morning she called me up and she said, "I couldn't put anything on the flag. I just had such a horrible night. I had terrible dreams—devils—I don't know what—horrible Bosch-like things—and I just was in such a strange mood I couldn't do anything." So then I gave it to a young woman who had been in my group in Poland who was now in New York, and I didn't tell her anything about any of this, and at about six o'clock in the morning she called me up and said, "I've got to come and see you right away." And I thought, "Oh, God." And so she came up, and she said, "I saw things—I saw things around the flag. Now, I know you're stubborn, and I know you want to take this thing with you, but if you'd follow my advice you'd put it in a hole in the ground and burn it and cover it with earth, because the devil's in it." So I never took the flag with me. In fact, I gave it to her, and she had a ceremony six months later in France with some friends in which they did burn it.

WALLY: God. That's really amazing. So did you ever go to India?

ANDRÉ: Yes, I went to India in the spring, and I came back home, Wally, feeling all wrong. You know, I mean, I'd been to India, and I'd just felt like a tourist. I'd found nothing. So I was spending the summer on Long Island with my family, and I heard about this community in Scotland called Findhorn where people sang and talked and meditated with plants.

WALLY: God—

ANDRÉ: And it was founded by several rather middle-class English and Scottish eccentrics—some of them intellectuals, and some of them not. And I heard that they grew things in soil that supposedly almost nothing could grow in because it's almost beach soil—and that they'd built—not built, they'd grown—er—the largest cauliflowers in the world—and there are sort of cabbages—they've supposedly grown trees which can't grow in the British Isles. And so I went there, and I mean, it is an amazing place, Wally. I mean, if there are insects bothering their plants, they will talk with the insects, and you know, make an agreement where they will set aside a special patch of vegetables just for the insects, and then the insects will leave the main part alone. And things like that. And they live with a sort of wild enthusiasm—you know, the word "enthusiasm" refers to "the god within," and they do somehow seem to see the god within everything. So all sorts of things that we would do sort of mechanically, just because we feel they have to be done, they do with an extraordinary intensity. I mean, for instance, all the buildings at Findhorn just shine. And then things like the icebox, the stove, the car—well, they all have names. And since you wouldn't treat Helen, the icebox, with any less respect than you would Margaret, your wife, you make sure that Helen is as clean as Margaret, or you know, is treated with the equal kind of respect, so that you— I saw, you know, on a day when the place was just filled with activity, the leaders of the community, this wonderful middle-class English couple, Peter and Eileen, they would stop, as the heads, or the inspiration, of this huge thing, and would do nothing but clean their car for five or six hours. And the car just looks supernatural, Wally, you see, it does. It glows. And the whole place glows, you see, for that reason, and that gives it a kind of magical aspect, and in that sense it is magic. They've discovered a new kind of magic. And when I was there, Wally—I remember being in the woods, and I would look at a leaf, and I would actually see that thing that was alive in that leaf, and then I remember just running through the woods as fast as I could, with this incredible laugh coming out of me, and really being in that state, you know, where laughter and tears seem to merge. And anyway, it just absolutely blasted me open. I mean,

when I came out of Findhorn I was hallucinating
nonstop. I was seeing clouds as creatures, the people
in the airplane all had animals' faces, I mean I was on
a trip.

WALLY: Uh-huh.

ANDRÉ: It was like being in a William Blake world suddenly. Things were exploding. And I immediately
went to Belgrade, because I wanted to talk to Grotowski. And so Grotowski and I got together at midnight in my hotel room in Belgrade, and we drank
instant coffee out of the top of my shaving cream,
and we talked from midnight till eleven the next
morning. And then we slept for three hours, and then
we had some lunch, and we talked from three in the
afternoon—I talked, he didn't say a word—three in
the afternoon until nine the next morning, and then
I caught an eleven o'clock plane out of Yugoslavia
and came back home.

WALLY: Gee.

ANDRÉ: After that I did a workshop here in New York—I
did a few workshops. But things were somehow end-
ing. And I guess really the last big event took place
that fall—it was out at Montauk on Long Island, and
there were only just about nine of us involved—
mostly men—and we borrowed Dick Avedon's property out at Montauk. And the country out there is
like Heathcliff country—it's absolutely wild. You
know, even in summer it's incredibly rugged. And
there's nothing on the property. It's just a small bush
forest, you know, with very high cliffs. And what we

wanted to do was to take the—to take All Souls' Eve, Halloween, and use it as a point of departure for something. And the idea was that each one of us would prepare something for the others, somehow in the spirit of All Souls' Eve. And we built ourselves this shack that we lived in, and it was getting very cold out there, you know, because it was November, late October. And the thing that I prepared was— I haven't had it for a while now, but I have a very, very unpleasant dream that my grandfather on my mother's side is still alive in a hotel room on the West Side. We haven't either known it or admitted it and haven't visited him all these years. And I visit him, and it's horrible, because I feel guilty. And so, since one of the ceremonies of All Souls' Eve is to welcome the dead, to bring the spirits of the dead that you love and to welcome them as you go into the dead of winter, I did something to try to bring my grandfather to peace. The others participated in it. But the big event was—three of the people kept disappearing in the middle of the night each night, and we knew they were preparing something big, but we didn't know what. And midnight on Halloween, under a dark moon, above these cliffs, we were all told to gather at the topmost cliff and that we would be taken somewhere. And we did. And it was cold, and we waited, and then the three of them—Helen, Bill, and Fred—showed up wearing white—something they'd made out of sheets that really looked a little spooky, not funny. And they took us into the ruined basement of a house that had burned down on the property. And in this basement they had set up a table with benches that they had made, and they had put out paper, pencils, wine, and glasses. And we were asked to sit at the table and make out our last will and testament, to think about and write down whatever our last words were to the world or to somebody we were close to. And that's quite a task. And we must have been there for about an hour and a half or so, maybe two. And one at a time they would ask one of us to come with them—suddenly a figure in white would appear and motion like this for one of us to come. So there were less and less people sitting at that table. And of course the longer you stayed, the harder it was, just thinking. But they gave everybody enough time to really have to somehow come to terms with it. And I was one of the last. And they came for me, and they put a blindfold on me, which is what they did—they did the same thing with everybody else—and they ran me through these fields—two people. And they had found what was a kind of potting shed—a kind of shed on the grounds, a little tiny room that had once had tools in it—and they took me down these stairs, and the room was *filled* with very harsh white light. And they told me to undress and give them all my valuables. Then they put me on a table, and they sponged me down. Now I started just flashing on death camps and secret police. I don't know what happened to the other people, but I started to cry uncontrollably. And then they stood me on my feet and took photographs of me naked. And then naked, again blindfolded, I was run through these forests again and thrown down into a kind of tent made of sheets, with sheets on the ground. And there were all these naked bodies huddling together for warmth in the cold. And we were left there for about an hour. And then one by one— again, one at a time—we were led out. The blindfold was put on, and I felt myself being lowered on to something like a stretcher. And the stretcher was carried a long way, very slowly, through the woods, and then I felt myself being lowered into the ground. They had in fact dug six graves, eight feet deep. And then I felt pieces of wood being put on me—I mean, I cannot tell you, Wally, what I was going through— and I was lowered into the grave on a stretcher, and then this wood was put on me, my valuables were put on me, in my hands, and they had stretched a sheet or canvas about this much above my head, and then they shoveled dirt onto the grave so that I really had the feeling of being buried alive. And after being in the grave for about half an hour—I mean, I didn't know how long I'd be in there—I was resurrected, lifted out of the grave, blindfold taken off, and run through the fields, and then we came to a great circle of fire with music and hot wine, and we danced till dawn. And at dawn we filled up the graves to the best of our ability and went back to New York.

WALLY: Wow. God.

Silence.

ANDRÉ: And that was really the last big event. That was the end. I mean, I began to realize that I just didn't want to do these things anymore. I felt sort of becalmed, like in that chapter in *Moby Dick* when the wind goes out of the sails. And you know, another strange thing was that I just couldn't imagine another event that would really be—I don't know—I just had the feeling that from now on I would always be able to foresee the outcome of these things—they wouldn't have that terrifying, exhilarating feeling of dropping into a black hole or whatever it was. They would become predictable—more like repertory theater or something. And I remember around this time going to this very strange magical island that's connected to Findhorn, where Macbeth was buried, where supposedly the last battle of Atlantis is still being fought, invisibly. And there were caves on the beach inhabited by hermits and wanderers, meditating and gazing out to sea. And I went into a church on the island to pray, because I was so confused, and in the middle of—I sort of walked in and started to pray, and then I got absolutely revolted, and I thought, I cannot pray anymore. This is revolting. No more prayer. No more magic. I've got to get out of this place. And then last winter without thinking about it very much I went to see an agent I know to tell him I was interested in directing plays again. Actually, he seemed a little surprised to see that Rip Van Winkle was still alive.

WALLY: Heh heh heh!

ANDRÉ: And it was strange. He sent me down to this theater to see a play—to see if I found the author interesting, you know. And it was a funny feeling suddenly sitting in the audience with Chiquita, looking at this play, and trying to make up my mind about it—I suddenly felt like an old hand, like an old pro, doing something professional. And I sat backstage with a couple of the actors afterward, and someone introduced me to some of the ones whom I'd never met before, and they'd heard about my work from the past, and I thought it was all very cozy, you know, that there was something terribly nice about that.

WALLY: God—yes—

ANDRÉ: Anyway—

Long silence. The WAITER *brings the main course.* WALLY *eats until* ANDRÉ'S *voice interrupts him.*

Yes, you know, frankly, I'm sort of repelled by the whole story, if you really want to know.

WALLY: What?

ANDRÉ: I mean, who did I think I was? You know? I mean, that's the story of some kind of spoiled princess. I mean, you know, who did I think I was, the Shah of Iran? I mean, you know, I wonder if people such as myself are not really Albert Speer, Wally. You know, Hitler's architect, Albert Speer?

WALLY: Wh—

ANDRÉ: Well, I've been thinking a lot about him recently. Because I think I am Speer. And I think it's time for me to be caught and tried the way he was.

WALLY: What are you talking about?

ANDRÉ: Well, he was a very cultivated man, an architect, an artist, so he thought the ordinary rules of life didn't apply to him. I mean, I would really like to be stripped and unmasked. I feel I deserve it. Because I really feel that everything I've done is horrific. Just horrific.

WALLY: My God—but why?

ANDRÉ: Well, you see—you see, I've seen a lot of death in these last few years, and there's one thing that's for sure about death. You do it alone. That seems really quite certain, you see, that I've seen, that—uh—that the people around your bed mean nothing. Your reviews mean nothing. Whatever it is, you do it alone. And so the question is, when I get on *my* deathbed, what kind of a person will I be. And I'm just very dubious about the kind of person who would have lived these last few years the way I did.

WALLY: Why should you feel that way?

ANDRÉ: Well, you see, I've had a very rough time in the last few months, Wally. Three different people in my family were in the hospital at the same time. Then my mother died. Then Marina had something wrong with her back, and we were terribly worried about her, although she's going to be all right, thank God. But I'm feeling very raw right now. I mean, I can't sleep, my nerves are shot—I feel like my face is being shoved in the mud—you know, I'm affected by everything. I mean, last week I had this really nice director from Norway over to dinner, and I've known him for years and years, and he's somebody that I *think* I'm very fond of, but I was just sitting there thinking that he was a pompous, defensive, conservative stuffed shirt who was only interested in the theater,

and he was talking and talking—and you see, his
mother was a famous Norwegian comedian—and I
realized that he had said "I remember my mother" at
least four hundred times during the evening, and he
was telling story after story about his mother—you
know, I had heard these stories twenty times before
—and he was drinking a whole bottle of bourbon,
very quietly, and his laugh was so horrible, you see, I
could hear his laugh, the pain in that laugh, the hol-
lowness—what being that woman's son had done to
him—

WALLY: Uh-huh—

ANDRÉ: —so that at a certain point I had to just ask him
to leave—you know, nicely—I just told him I had to
get up early the next morning—because it was so
horrible—it was just as if he had *died* in my living
room—and then I went into the bathroom and cried
because I had lost a friend. And then after he had
gone I turned the television on, and there was this
guy who had just won the something something—
some sports event—and he had won a great big check
and some kind of a huge silver bottle, and he couldn't
stuff the check into the bottle, somehow, and he
put the bottle in front of his nose and pretended it
was his face, and he wasn't really listening to the guy
who was interviewing him, but he was smiling ma-
levolently at his friends, and I looked at him and
thought, What a horrible, mean, empty, manipula-
tive rat, you know. And I thought, That guy is me.
And then *last* night it was actually our twentieth
wedding anniversary, and I took Chiquita to see this
show about Billie Holiday. And I just looked at

these show business people who know nothing about
Billie Holiday—nothing, you see—they were—they
were really kind of, in a way, intellectual creeps, and
suddenly I had this feeling—I mean, I was just sitting
there crying through most of the show, and suddenly
I had this feeling that I was just as creepy as they
were, and that my whole life had been a sham, and
that I didn't have the guts to be Billie Holiday either. I mean, I really feel I'm just washed up, wiped
out—I've just squandered my life.

WALLY: Gosh—André— How can you say something like
that?

They eat. Long silence.

ANDRÉ: But you know, I may be in a very emotional state
right now, but since I've come back home I've just
been finding the world we're living in more and more
upsetting. I mean, people here seem very very strange
to me now. I mean, I really find the people here very
very strange.

WALLY: I agree with you, but I'm always trying to figure
out how to describe just in what *way* they're strange.
Why would *you* say they're strange?

ANDRÉ: Well—all right. Well—last week I went down
to the Public Theater one afternoon, and when I
walked in I said hello to everybody, because I know
them all, and they all know me, and they're always
very friendly. And seven or eight people told me how
wonderful I looked. Then *one* person said to me—
one, a woman who runs the casting office, said, "Gee,

you look *horrible*. Is something wrong?" Now, she—
You know, we started talking, of course, I started
telling her things, and then she burst into tears because an aunt of hers who's eighty, whom she was
very fond of, went into the hospital for a cataract,
which was solved, but the nurse was so sloppy she
didn't put the bed rails up, and the aunt fell out of
bed and is now a complete cripple. So we were talking about hospitals. Now, this woman—because this
had happened to her very recently, and because of
who she is—she could see me with complete clarity.
She didn't know anything about what I'd been going
through. But the other people—what they saw was
this tan, or this shirt, or the fact that the shirt goes
well with the tan. And so they said, "Gee, you look
wonderful." Now, they're in an insane dream world.
They're not looking. Now that's very strange to me.

WALLY: Right. They didn't *see* anything, somehow, except
the few little things that they wanted to see.

ANDRÉ: It's like what happened just before my mother
died. You know, we had gone to the hospital to see
my mother, and I'd been in to see her, and I saw this
woman that looked as bad as any survivor of Ausch-
witz or Dachau, and I was out in the hall sort of
comforting my father, and this doctor who was a specialist in a problem that she had with her arm went
into her room and came out just beaming and said to
us, "Boy, don't *we* have a lot of reason to feel great?
Isn't that *wonderful* how she's coming along?" Well,
all he saw was the arm. That's all he saw. And I
mean, here's another person who's existing in a
dream. Who on top of that is a kind of butcher who's

committing a kind of familial murder, because he comes out of that room, and he psychically kills us by taking *us* into a dream world, you see, where we become confused and frightened, because the moment before, we saw somebody who looked already dead, and now here comes the specialist who tells us that everything is great. I mean, they were literally driving my father crazy, because here was an eighty-two-year-old man, who's very emotional, you know, and if you go in one minute, and you see that the person's dying, and you don't want them to die, and then a doctor comes out five minutes later and tells you they're in wonderful shape—uh, you know, you can go crazy.

WALLY: Right. I know. I know what you mean.

ANDRÉ: I mean, the doctor didn't see my mother. The people at the Public Theater didn't see me. We're all walking around in some kind of fog. I mean, I remember when something like all those school children in Belgium being kidnapped or the Munich massacre or the Guyana massacre would have absolutely stopped the world. I mean, people would have just stopped their work and listened to their radios. But that doesn't happen now. I don't know what's wrong. And another thing—I mean, maybe I just have this on my mind, Wally, but *I* think that we're living in the middle of a plague—that cancer today is of plague dimensions—which I find terrifying, because I'm terrified of cancer. Uh—and we know now that people in their twenties and thirties are being hit by it.

WALLY: Yes.

ANDRÉ: I mean, just since I've come back to New York, I've heard of half a dozen or a dozen cases—we hear it all the time. But is anybody calling it a plague? I mean, in the time of the Black Plague, when the plague hit, people got the hell out. The whole English court left London. Anybody who could get on the roads went. People knew you should *get out!* Now—uh—say you believe that what we're doing to the environment contributes to cancer—and you know, the chemicals we use, the food we eat—what are we doing about it? Are we doing anything? You know, when the plague hit, people put handkerchieves over their noses. But what are *we* doing? I think we're all in a trance. We're walking around like zombies. I mean, I don't think we're even aware of ourselves or of our own reactions to things. I mean, like with the Norwegian director, what would be the normal thing that we all would do now would be that I would have spent the evening with him and then when Chiquita came back I would have said, "Oh, I had such a nice cozy evening," and "Oh, we had such an interesting talk about Norway," and so on, even though actually I was absolutely miserable, and I found this man's company unbearable. You know, if you *admit* to yourself that you just spent an evening with someone and for some reason or another on that particular evening they were somehow driving you insane, then I think you immediately begin to feel some kind of sympathy for that person, and you begin to wonder how he came to be in the state he's in. But we don't admit those things to ourselves. We just bottle everything up. I mean, really, we're just going around all day like unconscious machines, and meanwhile there's all this rage and worry and uneasiness just building up and building up inside us.

WALLY: Yes, that's right. They build up, and then they *leap out* inappropriately. I mean, I remember when I was in this play based on *The Master and Margarita* by Bulgakov, and I was playing the part of the cat, but they had trouble making up my cat suit, so in fact I didn't get it all delivered to me until the night of the first performance. Particularly the head—I'd never even had a chance to try it on. And about four of my fellow actors actually came up to me and said things which I just couldn't help thinking were attempts to destroy me. You know, one of them said, "Oh, that head will totally change your *hearing* in the performance. You'll hear everything *completely differently,* and it may be *very upsetting.* Why, I was once in a performance where I was wearing ear muffs, and I couldn't hear anything anybody said." And then another actor said, "Oh, you know, whenever I wear even a *hat* on stage, I tend to *faint.*" I mean, those remarks were just full of hostility, because, you know, if I'd listened to those people, I would have gone out there on stage, and I wouldn't have been able to hear anything, and I would have fainted. But the hostility was completely inappropriate, because in fact those people liked me. I mean, the hostility was some feeling left over from some previous experience. Because somehow in our social existence we're *only* allowed to express our feelings weirdly and indirectly. If you express them directly, everyone goes crazy.

ANDRÉ: Did you express *your* feelings about what those people said to you?

WALLY: No! I mean, I didn't *really* even know what I felt

until I thought about it later. And even if I *had* known what I felt—I mean, at the most, in a situation like that, I might say something, if I'm *really* annoyed, like, "Yes, well that's just fascinating, and I probably *will* faint tonight, just as you did."

ANDRÉ: Yeah. That's very baroque. That person wouldn't know what the hell you were saying to him. I do just the same thing.

WALLY: I mean, it's just not easy to do anything else. I mean, do you remember—I remember a party we both went to years ago somewhere over on Park Avenue in around the eighties, I think. And you were there, and Debby and I were there, and it was just in that period after Nixon resigned when for some reason *nobody* talked about anything political for any reason. I mean, it was just taboo. It was just not done. And at one point during the evening you started talking about something having to do with the politics of the moment—the international situation—I don't remember exactly what it was—and you became quite serious, and you were all of a sudden saying just a few things that were quite impassioned and that you really meant. And everybody went practically insane.

ANDRÉ: Really?

WALLY: Yes—I remember it was as if six people just rushed up to stop you and to—to put you back in—your cage or something. It was as if something uncanny had happened. You know, everyone started making jokes and acting as if of course you didn't mean it, and everyone was talking at once. And even in my own way, I was also pushed back, because I said a couple of things.

ANDRÉ: Yes, I remember that. That's right.

WALLY: Just as soon as you got serious, suddenly everyone else was *joking*—

ANDRÉ: Well, look—I remember a night— It was about two weeks after my mother died, and I was in pretty bad shape, and I went out to dinner with three relatively close friends, two of whom had known my mother quite well, and all three of whom have known me for years. And we went through that entire evening without my being able to, for a moment, get anywhere near what—you know, not that I wanted to sit and have a dreary evening in which I was talking about all this pain that I was going through and everything—really not at all. But—but the fact that nobody could say, Gee, what a shame about your mother, or How are you feeling? But it was as if nothing had happened. And everyone was just making these jokes and laughing. And I got actually quite crazy, as a matter of fact, and one of these people mentioned a certain man whom I don't like very much, and I started screeching about how he had just been found in the Bronx River, and his penis had dropped off from gonorrhea, and all kinds of insane things—and of course I realized when I got home that I'd just been desperate to break through this ice.

WALLY: Yeah—

ANDRÉ: I mean, do you realize, Wally, if you brought that situation into a Tibetan home, that would be just *so far out*—

WALLY: Right—

ANDRÉ: They wouldn't be able to understand it.

WALLY: Right.

ANDRÉ: I mean, that would be simply so weird, if four Tibetans came together, and tragedy had just struck one of the ones, and they all spent the whole evening going *Aha ha ha ehee hee hee oho ho! Wo—ho ho ho!* Those Tibetans would have looked at that and would have thought it was just the most unimaginable behavior, but for us that's common behavior. I mean, really—uh—the Africans would have probably put their spears into all four of us because it would have driven them crazy. They would have thought we were dangerous animals or something like that.

WALLY: Right.

ANDRÉ: You know, that's absolutely abnormal behavior.

The WAITER *approaches the table.*

WAITER: Is everything all right, gentlemen?

ANDRÉ, WALLY: Fine, thank you. . . .

The WAITER *pours wine.*

ANDRÉ: But these are typical evenings for us. We go to
parties or dinners like that all the time. And these
evenings are really like sort of sickly dreams, because
people are talking in symbols—everyone is sort of
floating through this fog of symbols and unconscious
feelings: No one says what they're really thinking
about; they don't talk *to* each other; because I think
people are really in some sort of state of fear or panic
about the world we're living in, but they don't know
it, and so you just hear these odd lines of dialogue
that seem to come from nowhere: you know, someone will be attacking some movie they saw or some
article they read—someone else will be talking about
crime in New York or the subways or something—
someone else will be shouting about what a terrible
time they're having at the party itself—and then people will start making these jokes that are really some
sort of secret code—

WALLY: Right—well, what often happens in some of these
evenings is that people will start spinning these really
crazy little fantasies, and everyone will be talking at
once and saying, you know, Wouldn't it be great if
Frank Sinatra and Mrs. Nixon and blah blah blah
were in such and such a situation—you know, always
with famous people, and always sort of grotesque. Or
people will be talking about some horrible thing like
the death of the girl in the car with Ted Kennedy
and just roaring with laughter. I mean, it's really
amazing. It's unbelievable. I mean, that's the only
way anything is expressed—through these completely
insane jokes. That may be why I never understand
what's going on at a party, and I'm always completely
confused. I mean, we'll come home, and Debby will

describe some incredible incident, and I won't have
even noticed it. Everything passes in a kind of trance.
You know, Debby once said after one of these New
York evenings that she thought she'd traveled a
greater distance just by journeying from her origins in
the suburbs of Chicago to that New York evening
than her grandmother had traveled in making her
way from the steppes of Russia to the suburbs of
Chicago.

ANDRÉ: I think that's right. What we *need* is to analyze
our situation in the world with great clarity, so that
we can act and respond appropriately, but instead,
when we get together, we fall into a kind of collective
hysteria, in which nobody knows what's going on.
And I mean, it may be, Wally, that one of the reasons that we *don't* know what's going on is that when
we're there at one of these parties we're all too busy
performing. We're concentrating on playing our own
roles and giving a good performance, so we *can't* perceive what's going on around us. That was one of the
reasons Grotowski gave up the theater, you know. He
just felt that people in their lives now were performing so well that performance in the theater was sort
of superfluous and in a way obscene. I mean, isn't it
amazing how often a doctor will live up to our expec-
tation of how a doctor should look, and when you see
a terrorist on television he looks just like a terrorist? I
mean, we live in a world in which fathers or single
people or artists are all trying to live up to someone's
fantasy of how a father or a single person or an artist
should look and behave. And so everyone acts as if
they know exactly how they ought to conduct themselves at every single moment, and they all seem to-

tally self-confident. Of course, privately, people are very mixed up about themselves, you know, and don't know *what* they should be doing in their lives, and they're reading all these self-help books—

WALLY: Right. And I mean, these books are so touching, because they show how desperately curious we are to know how all the others of us are really getting on in life, even though by performing these roles all the time we're hiding the reality of *ourselves* from everyone else. You know, we do live in ludicrous ignorance of each other. I mean, we usually don't know the things we'd like to know even about our supposedly closest friends. I mean, suppose you're going through some kind of hell in your own life, well, you would *love* to know if your friends have experienced similar things. But we really don't dare to ask each other.

ANDRÉ: No. It would be like asking your friend to drop his role.

WALLY: We just put no value at all on perceiving reality. On the contrary, the incredible emphasis we place now on our so-called careers automatically makes perceiving reality a very low priority, because if your life is organized around trying to be successful in a career, then it just doesn't matter what you perceive or what you experience. You're just thinking, Well, have I done the thing that I've planned? Have I performed this necessary action for my career? And so you really can sort of shut your mind off for years ahead in a way. You can sort of turn on the automatic pilot. Just the way your mother's doctor had on his automatic pilot when he went in and looked at the arm and totally failed to perceive anything else.

ANDRÉ: Right. Our minds are just focused on these goals and plans, which in themselves are not reality.

WALLY: No. Goals and plans are not reality. They're fantasy. They're part of a dream life. And you know, it always does seem so *ridiculous*, somehow, that everybody has to have his little goal in life. It's so absurd in a way. I mean, when you consider that it doesn't matter which one it is. I mean, I guess maybe it's satisfying to devote your life to trying to get money, or trying to create great works of art. I don't know. But when they're so interchangeable, somehow it seems sort of pathetic.

ANDRÉ: Yeah, it does.

WALLY: But we just seem to think today that the person who pursues his goals most single-mindedly and fanatically is the person most worthy of respect. I mean, I think maybe that's why actors are not given a great deal of respect: it's because actors spend most of their time actually playing, like children. I mean, each night when I was putting on my fake nose during the fourth act of *The Mandrake*, I would think about the fact that, when I was growing up, this wasn't what people had in mind for me. But I mean, there's always the excuse for an actor that, you know, you may be putting on a fake nose and running around acting like a jerk, but then after the performance you can hang up your nose and you can put on a suit and tie, and, you know, in England you can even be a lord and be quite a distinguished member of society, or Charlton Heston, you know, can be a very important member of the National Endowment for the Arts and things like that—you can really act like a businessman.

ANDRÉ: Right. The actor hangs up his nose and puts on a suit, and you know, I think businessmen do just the opposite—they take off their suits and put on a nose. I mean, you know, they need to play too, so they go out drinking or carousing or whatever it is. I mean, the man who becomes a businessman has a difficult life. He has to go to work every day. For us that's very exotic. He has to sit up in the penthouse of some skyscraper all day seriously talking about stocks. And I think that people like us are what Jung would call his shadow side. We are who part of him would like to be, just as part of us would like to be having those luncheons, making that money, wheeling and dealing and so on.

WALLY: You're darn right. But playing takes people away from this focus on their goals, so it's considered contemptible.

ANDRÉ: And then, because people's concentration is on their goals, in their life they just live each moment by habit, really, just like the Norwegian telling the same stories over and over. Life becomes habitual. And it is, today. I mean, you know, very few things happen now like when Marlon Brando sent the Indian woman to accept the Oscar and everything went haywire.

WALLY: Right.

ANDRÉ: Things just very rarely go haywire now.

WALLY: Right.

ANDRÉ: And if you're just operating by habit, then you're not really living. I mean, you know, in Sanskrit, the root of the verb "to be" is the same as "to grow" or "to make grow."

WALLY: Right.

Pause.

ANDRÉ: I mean, do you know about Roc?

WALLY: About what?

ANDRÉ: Roc of Findhorn?

WALLY: No.

ANDRÉ: Oh, well, Roc was a wonderful man. And you know, he was one of the founders of Findhorn—

WALLY: Uh-huh—

ANDRÉ:—and he was one of Scotland's—well, he *was* Scotland's greatest mathematician, and one of the century's great mathematicians, and he prided himself on the fact that he had no dream life, no fantasy life, nothing to stand between—no imaginary life—nothing to stand between him and the direct perception of mathematics. And when he was in his mid-fifties, he was walking in the gardens of Edinburgh, and he saw a faun, and the faun was very surprised because fauns have always been able to see people, but very few people ever see them. And—you know, the little imaginary creatures? Not a deer—

WALLY: Oh.

ANDRÉ: You call them fauns, don't you?

WALLY: Oh. I thought a fawn was a baby deer—

ANDRÉ: Yeah, well, there's a deer that's called a fawn. But these are—these are like—those little—

WALLY: Oh—the kind that Debussy—er—uh—

ANDRÉ: Yes, right. Well, anyway, he got to know the faun, and then he got to know other fauns, and a series of conversations began, and more and more fauns would come every afternoon to meet him, and he'd have talks with the fauns, and then one day, after a while, when, you know, they'd really gotten to know him, they asked him if he would like to meet Pan, because Pan would like to meet him, and of course Pan was afraid of terrifying him because he knew the Christian misconception which portrayed Pan as an evil creature, which he's not, but Roc said he would love to meet Pan, and so they met, and Pan indirectly sent him on his way on a journey in which he met the other people who began Findhorn. But Roc used to practice certain exercises, like, for instance, if he were right-handed, all today he would do everything with his left hand. All day—writing, eating, everything—opening doors—in order to break the habits of living, because the great danger for him, he felt, was to fall into a trance, out of habit. And he had a whole series of exercises, very simple ones, that he invented to just keep seeing, feeling, remembering. Because, you see, you have to *learn* now—it didn't used to be necessary, but today you have to *learn* something like, Are you really hungry? or are you just stuffing your face because that's what—what you do, out of habit? I mean, you can afford to do it, so you do it, whether you're hungry or not. Now, if you go to the Buddhist Meditation Center, they make you taste each bite of your food so that it takes about two hours—it's horrible—to eat your lunch. But you're conscious of the taste of the food. If you're just eating out of habit, you *don't* taste the food, and you're not in touch with the reality of what's happening to you; you're in a dream world again.

WALLY: Right. Well, do you think maybe we're living in this dream world because we do so many things every day that somehow affect us in ways we're not aware of? I mean, I was thinking, for example, now, last Christmas, Debby and I were given an electric blanket. And I can tell you that it's such a marvelous advance over our former way of life, and it's great. But it's quite different from *not* having an electric blanket, and I sometimes sort of wonder, well, what is it doing to me? I mean, I sort of feel—I'm not sleeping quite in the same way.

ANDRÉ: No, you wouldn't be.

WALLY: I mean, and my dreams are sort of different, and I feel a little bit different when I get up in the morning.

ANDRÉ: Well, I wouldn't put an electric blanket on for anything.

WALLY: Uh-huh.

ANDRÉ: First, I'd be worried that I might get electrocuted. I don't trust technology. But I mean, the main thing, Wally, is that that kind of comfort just separates you from reality in a very direct way.

WALLY: You mean—

ANDRÉ: I mean, if you *don't* have that electric blanket and your apartment is cold—

WALLY: Uh-huh—

ANDRÉ: —and you need to put on another blanket, or go into the closet and pile up coats on top of the blankets you have, well, then, you *know* it's cold.

WALLY: Right.

ANDRÉ: And that sets up a link of things. You have compassion for the person—is the person *next* to you cold? Are there other people in the world who are cold? What a cold night! I *like* the cold. My God, I don't really want a blanket—I never realized—it's *fun* being cold! I can snuggle up against you even more because it's cold— All sorts of things occur to you.

But, turn on that electric blanket, and it's like taking a tranquilizer, or it's like being lobotomized by watching television. I think you enter the dream world again. I mean, what does it do to us, Wally, to live in an environment where something as massive as the seasons and the cold and the winter don't in any way affect us? Because we're animals, after all. I mean, what does that mean? That means that instead of living under the sun and the moon and the sky and the stars, we're living in a fantasy world of our own making.

WALLY: Yes, but I mean, I would *never* give up my electric blanket, André, because New York is cold, our apartment is cold in the winter. It's a difficult environment. Our lives are tough enough as it is. I mean, I'm not trying to get rid of the few things that provide relief and comfort. On the contrary, I'm looking for *more* comfort, because the world is very abrasive. I mean, I'm trying to protect myself, because really there are these abrasive beatings to be avoided, everywhere you look.

ANDRÉ: But, Wally, don't you see that comfort can be dangerous? I mean, you like to be comfortable, and I like to be comfortable too, but don't you see that comfort can lull you into a dangerous tranquillity? I mean, my mother knew a woman, Lady Hatfield, who was one of the richest women in the world, but she died of starvation because all she would eat was chicken. I mean, she just liked chicken, Wally, and that was all she would eat, and actually her body was starving, but she didn't know it, because she was quite happy eating her chicken, and so she finally died. You see, I honestly believe we're all like Lady Hatfield now. We're having a lovely, comfortable time with our electric blankets and our chicken, and meanwhile we're starving, because we're so cut off from contact with reality that we're not getting any real sustenance. Because we don't see the world. We don't see ourselves. We don't see how our actions affect other people. You know, Kozan would get terribly upset if I'd be fifteen minutes late for an appointment. And he would say, "You made a promise. You've broken your promise." Because we don't take our commitments seriously. We don't think about what we're saying and doing. I mean, there was this thing that happened to me when I was visiting Warsaw last year—because I've been back a couple of times since the time I told you about—

WALLY: Uh-huh—

ANDRÉ: I was attending this conference that was run by the ITI—the International Theater Institute—and at one point I decided that I wanted to go out and join this extraordinary group I'd heard about who worked in the country, in villages that haven't been changed since the time of the Hundred Years' War.

WALLY: Right.

ANDRÉ: Now, at that point the ITI conference was over, but I happened to be at the ITI office, and there was a young man there who was just locking up the office. He was about twenty-five or something like that, twenty-six. And I grabbed this guy, and I said, "Listen"—and I'd never met him or anything, but he knew me because I'd been in and out of the office—

and his work for ITI was over, so he had nothing to gain—and I said, "Listen, you know, I'm going to go work with this group, and I know I'll need a sleeping bag, and I didn't bring one to Poland with me. You don't know where I could borrow one, do you?" And he said, "Oh, you can borrow mine, that's no problem." And he said, "Meet me in the bar tonight at eleven, and I'll bring it to you." And I said, "Wonderful." And I went to the bar, and he didn't show up. Midnight came, one o'clock. So, you know, I figured what one would here. It didn't mean anything to him, and he'd forgotten about it. So the next day I got on this train, and I went on what was a four-hour journey by train and then an hour and a half journey by bus, and then an hour on foot. This was really far away. And four or five hours after I arrived, he arrived, with the sleeping bag.

WALLY: No!

ANDRÉ: He hadn't been able to keep the appointment because his mother hadn't been well, and he'd tried to get hold of me, and he'd made a promise, and he had hitchhiked all this way just to give me the sleeping bag.

WALLY: God, that's incredible.

ANDRÉ: Now, I don't think that could happen with us here. I'm not really sure why, but I just can't picture it.

WALLY: I know. I agree with you. Somehow we're just not—I mean, I don't know why this occurs to me, but it somehow reminds me of— When I was acting in

The Master and Margarita at the Public Theater, the role of the devil was played by a wonderful Czech actor named Jan Triska. And I was always incredibly struck by the way that he would say good evening to each of his fellow actors, you know, as we would be arriving for the evening's performance and starting to get dressed. I mean, it was the *way* he would greet us—it was just so *respectful* somehow—it was as if we were all dignified members of some very highly disciplined and honorable organization. I don't know how to describe it, but he seemed to take us all so seriously, and it was as if putting on this performance really was something that mattered, something special, something with some kind of sacred quality.

ANDRÉ: Well, that's like that Hasidic thing, Wally—that Hasidic idea of making every moment a sacrament, a gift, or an act of veneration. I mean, Wally, have you read Martin Buber's book *On Hasidism?*

WALLY: No.

ANDRÉ: Well, here's a view of life— I mean, he talks about the belief of the Hasidic Jews that there are spirits chained in everything—there are spirits chained in you, there are spirits chained in me, there are spirits chained in this table—and that prayer is the action of liberating these enchained embryo-like spirits, and that every action of ours in life—whether it's doing business or making love or having dinner together or whatever—that every action should be a prayer, a sacrament, in the world. Now do you think we're living like that?

WALLY: No—

ANDRÉ: Now why do you think we're not living like that? I think it's because if we allowed ourselves to see what we're doing every day, we might find it just too nauseating. I mean, the way we treat other people—I mean, you know, every day, several times a day, I walk into my apartment building. The doorman calls me Mr. Gregory, and I call him Jimmy. The same transaction probably occurs between you and the guy you buy groceries from every day, in some other way.

WALLY: Uh-huh.

ANDRÉ: Now already, what is the difference between that and the Southern plantation owner who's got slaves? You see, I think that an act of murder is committed in that moment, when I walk into my building. Because here is a dignified, intelligent man, a man of my own age, and when I call him Jimmy, then he becomes a child, and I'm an adult. Because I can buy my way into that building. And I remember an elevator man who every single night used to give me the weather report—I mean, that was all he could talk about. No matter what you said to him, he gave you the weather report—now I think that that man had been murdered inside that elevator by people like me.

WALLY: Right. That's right. I mean, my God, when I was a Latin teacher, people used to treat *me*—I mean, if I would go to a party of professional or literary people, I mean, I was just treated—uh—in the nicest sense of the word, like a dog. In other words, there was no *question* of my being able to participate on an equal basis in the conversation with people. I mean, I would occasionally *have* conversations with people, but then when they asked what I did, which would always happen after about five minutes—uh, you know, their faces—even if they were enjoying the conversation, or they were flirting with me or whatever it was—their faces would just, you know, have that expression like the portcullis crashing down, you know, those medieval gates—

ANDRÉ: Heh heh—

WALLY: —and they would just walk away. I mean, I literally lived like a dog. I mean, you know, I would be at a party where there would be all these great personalities, and the idea that I could participate in things in any way except to sort of pad through on all fours and sort of lick people's trousers was just inconceivable.

ANDRÉ: God. That's right.

WALLY: And I mean, when Debby was working as a secretary, you know, if she would tell people what she did, they would just go insane. I mean, they just wouldn't be able to handle it. You know, it would be as if she'd said—uh—"Well, you know, I'm serving a life sentence for child murdering." And I mean, you know, when you talk about our attitudes toward people—I mean, you know, I think of myself as a very decent, good person simply because I think I'm reasonably friendly to most of the people I happen to meet every day. I mean, I really think of myself quite smugly, and I think I'm a perfectly nice guy, so long as I somehow think of the world as consisting of, you know, just the small circle of the people I know as friends—or just the few people that we know in this little world of our hobbies—the theater or whatever it is. And I'm really quite self-satisfied. I'm happy with myself. I have no complaint about myself. I mean, if I'm just one more nice student in the Dalton School in the seventh grade, well then, you know, I'm just as nice as the next guy in the seventh grade. But the thing is, you know, let's face it, there's a whole enormous world out there that I don't ever think about, and I *certainly* don't take responsibility for how I've lived in *that* world. I mean, if I were actually to confront the fact that I'm sort of sharing this stage with the starving person in Africa somewhere, well then I wouldn't feel so great about myself. So naturally I blot those people out of my perception. So of course I'm ignoring a whole section of the real world. You know, Hannah Arendt was always writing about the fact that the more involved you are in corruption or evil, and the more areas of your own existence there are that you therefore don't want to think about, or that you can't face, or that you have to lie about, the more distorted your perception of reality will be in general. (*Pause.*) In other words, we all have every reason to hide from reality, and it's a terrible problem. But I mean, frankly, when I write a play, in a way one of the things I guess I'm trying to do is precisely to bring myself up against some little bits of reality, and I'm trying to share that with an audience. (*Pause.* ANDRÉ *says nothing.*) I mean, the theater—I mean, of course we all know that the theater is in terrible shape today. I mean, you know, at least a few years ago people who really cared about the theater used to say, "The theater is dead." But now everyone has redefined the theater in such a trivial way. You know, I mean, I know people who are involved with the theater who go to see things now that—I mean, a few years ago these same people would have just been *embarrassed* to have even *seen* some of these plays—I mean, they would have just *shrunk*, you know, just in *horror*, at the superficiality of these things. But *now* they say, "Oh, that was pretty good." It's just incredible. And I just find that attitude unbearable, because I actually do believe that the theater can be very important—it can actually help people come in contact with reality. Now you may not feel that at all. You may find that absurd.

ANDRÉ: But, Wally, don't you see the dilemma? You're not taking into account the period we live in! I mean, of *course* that's what the theater *should* do. I've always felt that! I mean, when I was a young director, and I directed *The Bacchae* at Yale, *my* impulse, when Pentheus has been killed by his mother and the Furies, and you know, they pull the tree back and they tie him to the tree, and they fling him into the air, and he flies through space and he's killed, and they rip him to shreds and I guess cut off his head—*my* impulse was that the thing to do was to get a head from the New Haven morgue and pass it around the audience. I wanted Agawe to bring on a real head and that the head should be passed around the audience so that people somehow realized that this stuff was real, see. That it's real stuff. But the actress playing Agawe absolutely refused to do it. Well, I wouldn't do it myself today, but that was my impulse at the time. And I still think it would be wonderful if the perceptions of the audience could be brought to life, if the senses of the audience could be brought to life. You know, Gordon Craig used to talk about why is there gold and silver in the churches or something—the great cathedrals—when *actors* could be wearing gold and silver? And I mean, people who saw Eleanora Duse in the last couple of years of her life, Wally—people said it was like seeing light on stage, or mist, or the essence of something. I mean, people don't talk about it as performance or acting; they said it was like the backgrounds of certain da Vinci paintings or something like that. And then when you think of Bertolt Brecht—he did something that was perhaps the most amazing thing of all. You know, he somehow created a theater in which people could observe, that was vastly entertaining and exciting, but in which the excitement didn't overwhelm you. I mean, he managed to allow you the distance between the play and yourself that in fact two human beings need in order to live together. You know, people say that he was against feeling, but that's just not true. *I* think he was looking for a kind of clarity in the theater that would permit *real* feeling, and what I think he was *against* was that kind of feverish intensity of emotion that erupts when *real* feeling is suppressed. But, Wally, the question is whether the theater *now* can do for an audience what Brecht tried to do or what Craig or Duse tried to do. Can it do it now? Because, you see, I think people are so deeply asleep today that unless you're putting on those sort of superficial plays that help your audience to sleep more comfortably, I think it's very hard to know what to do in the theater. I mean, what if those people in the audience aren't just asleep? What if they're dead? So that nothing you can *do* on the stage will wake them up? I mean, the last season my

company performed in New York, I remember thinking something was very wrong. You know, there we
were, and the actors were doing excellent work, and
all of a sudden it began to feel as if we were performing in some gigantic opera house, and every member
of the audience was sitting in the back row, and I just
began to feel that there was nothing we could do to
reach those people.

WALLY: So you were trying to bring the patient back to
life—

ANDRÉ: Right.

WALLY: And you know, you performed Chekhov in front
of the patient, and it didn't work.

ANDRÉ: Right. Exactly.

WALLY: So you just did every play you could think of, and
then finally you just picked that person up and put
him over your back and carried him off to the Hima-
layas and put him on Mount Everest, just to see if
that would do it.

ANDRÉ: That's right. That's right. He had to go to Mount
Everest. It was another form of theater. Because I
mean, you know, when we were lying in those graves,
a part of us believed we were really being buried
alive, and a part of us knew we weren't, just the way
in the theater a part of you believes people are really
being murdered on stage, and yet you know they're
not. It *was* theater, because we were consciously
creating an intense imaginative experience for one

another. We weren't *really* burying each other alive; we were playing. And in things like that beehive, we might have had impulses to kill each other or to make love, just as actors do in rehearsals, but we didn't, because it wasn't life, it was theater. But it wasn't the kind of theater in which an audience passively watches a *play*. I mean, not that there's anything wrong with plays. Plays are great. But what kind of plays are appropriate today? It's very confusing. Because, for instance—for instance, I think that if you put on serious contemporary plays by writers like yourself, you may only be helping to deaden the audience in a different way. I mean, there was a time when contemporary plays of a certain kind would have had a prophetic function and would have been *warnings* to people, but now I think there has been *such* a degeneration, and the world is *so* dark and cold, that even those works which once were outcries *against* the darkness can now only contribute to the deadening process.

WALLY: What do you mean?

ANDRÉ: Well, Wally, how do you think it affects an audience to put on one of these plays in which you show that people are totally isolated now, and they can't reach other, and their lives are obsessive and driven and desperate? Or how does it affect them to see a play that shows that our world is full of nothing but shocking sexual events and violence and terror? Does that help to wake up a sleeping audience? You see, I don't think so, because I think it's very likely that the picture of the world that you're showing them in a play like that is exactly the picture of the world that they have already. You know, they *know* their own lives and relationships are painful and difficult, and if they watch the evening news on television, well there what they see is a terrifying chaotic universe full of rapes and murders and hands cut off by subway cars and children pushing their parents out of windows. So the play simply tells them that their impression of the world is correct, and there's absolutely no way out, there's nothing they can do. They end up feeling passive and impotent. And so the experience has helped to deaden them. They're more asleep than when they went into the theater. I mean, I love the theater, Wally, I want to direct plays again, but it's very difficult, because the things that I'd like to do in the theater . . . I mean, look at something like that christening that my group arranged for me in the forest in Poland. Well, there was an example of people creating something that really had all the elements of theater. It was worked on carefully, it was thought about carefully, it was done with exquisite taste and magic, and they in fact created something—which in this case was in a way just for an audience of one, just for me—they in fact created something that had ritual, love, surprise, denouement, beginning, middle, and end—and it had a real moon instead of a painted moon and a real castle instead of a painted castle, but it was an incredibly beautiful piece of theater. And the impact it had on its audience, on me, was somehow a totally positive one. It didn't deaden me, it brought me to life.

WALLY: But, André, are you saying that it's impossible—I mean, really—I mean, isn't it a little upsetting to come to the conclusion that there's no way to wake people up anymore except to involve them in some kind of christening in Poland or some kind of strange experience on top of Mount Everest? Because I mean —the awful thing is—let's face it, André—I mean, if you say that it really is necessary to take everybody to Everest, then it's really tough, because everybody can't be taken to Everest. I mean, there must have been periods in history when you would have been able to save the patient through less drastic measures. I mean, there must have been periods when in order to give people a strong or meaningful experience you wouldn't actually have to take them to Everest.

ANDRÉ: But you do now. In some way or other, you do now.

WALLY: I mean, there was a time when you could have just, for instance, written—I don't know—*Sense and Sensibility* by Jane Austen, and I'm sure that the people who read it had a pretty strong experience. I'm sure they did. All right, now you're saying that people today wouldn't get it. And maybe that's true. But I mean, isn't there any kind of writing or any kind of play that—I mean, isn't it legitimate for writers still to try to portray reality so that people can see it? . . . I mean, of *course* the things you did in those workshops had a powerful impact on you. I mean, you know, they weren't really aesthetic experiences, they were just experiences in your life. I mean, if you find yourself buried in a grave, obviously it affects you. And I mean, the whole thing about those workshops was that you obviously weren't *allowed* to have any sort of ordinary, daily experiences. You know, you say that people followed their impulses, but I'm sure it would have been sort of frowned on if somebody had just stood up one day and started saying, "Well, my career is going great, I've really had a great year, I'm making more money than you are," or something like that. And I'm sure it would have been frowned on if somebody had just gone to the library in Warsaw and taken out a book and brought it into the room and started to read it. . . . But I mean, the main thing, André, is, why do we require a trip to Mount Everest in order to be able to perceive one moment of reality? Is Mount Everest more real than New York? Isn't New York real? I mean, I think if you could become fully aware of what existed in the cigar store next door to this restaurant, it would blow your brains out. I mean, isn't there just as much reality to be perceived in a cigar store as there is on Mount Everest? What do you think? I mean, *I* think that not only is there nothing more real about Mount Everest, *I* think there's nothing that *different*, in a certain way. I mean, reality is sort of uniform, in a way. So that if your perceptions are—I mean, if your—if your own mechanism is—is operating correctly, it would become irrelevant to go to Mount Everest, and sort of absurd, because—uh—ha ha—it just—I mean, of course—I mean, on some level—obviously it's very different from a cigar store on Seventh Avenue, but—I mean—

ANDRÉ: Well, I agree with you, Wally, but the problem is that people *can't see* the cigar store now. I mean, things don't affect people the way they used to. I mean, it may very well be that in another ten years people will pay ten thousand dollars in cash to be castrated, just in order to be affected by something.

WALLY: Well, why do you think that is? Why is that? Is it just because people are lazy today, or they're bored? You know, when children are poor and they live in the country and have just a few little things to play with, then they're very, very thrilled by those few little things. But if they're rich and live in the city and have a thousand things to play with, then they always seem to be bored, and it's impossible to find anything to interest them.

ANDRÉ: Well, the word "spoiled" isn't a chance word, it's a strong word.

WALLY: Yeah.

ANDRÉ: To be spoiled.

WALLY: Right. In other words, there's just—they're lost, in that sense. I mean, "spoiled" means, you know—I mean, a piece of meat that's been spoiled can't be unspoiled. It's doomed.

ANDRÉ: Right.

WALLY: So I mean, is that our problem? Is that what you're saying? Are we just like bored, spoiled children who've been lying in the bathtub all day, playing with their plastic duck, and now they're thinking, What can I do?

ANDRÉ: Okay. Yes. We're bored now. We're all bored. But has it ever occurred to you, Wally, that the process which creates this boredom that we see in the world now may very well be a self-perpetuating unconscious form of brainwashing created by a world totalitarian government based on money? And that all of this is much more dangerous, really, than one thinks? And that it's not just a question of individual survival, Wally, but that somebody who's bored is asleep? And somebody who's asleep will not say no?

WALLY: Uh-huh—

ANDRÉ: You see, I keep meeting these people—I mean, I was talking a few days ago with a man I greatly admire—he's a Swedish physicist, Gustav Björnstrand—and he told me that he no longer watches television, he doesn't read the newspapers, and he doesn't read magazines. He's completely cut them out of his life because he really does feel we're living in some kind of Orwellian nightmare now, and that everything that you hear now contributes to turning you into a robot. Because there's no doubt about it—we *are* becoming robots. Everyone on the outside can see this. I mean, I had dinner with two European friends of mine the other night, and they used to *love* New York. And they said everybody had turned into robots here—*everybody*—and the food was robot food, and you said something to people, and you really didn't get a response. They said New York had become like a morgue. And when I was at Findhorn I met this extraordinary English tree expert who had devoted his life to saving trees, and he'd just got back from Washington lobbying to save the redwoods. And he was eighty-four years old, and he always travels with a backpack because he never knows where he's going to be tomorrow. And when I met him at Findhorn he said to me, "Where are you from?" And I said, "New

York." And he said, "Ah, New York, yes, that's a very interesting place. Do you know a lot of New Yorkers who keep talking about the fact that they want to leave, but never do?" And I said, "Oh, yes." And he said, "Why do you think they don't leave?" And I gave him different banal theories. And he said, "Oh, I don't think it's that way at all." He said, "I think that New York is the new model for the new concentration camp, where the camp has been built by the inmates themselves, and the inmates are the guards, and they have this pride in this thing that they've built—they've built their own prison—and so they exist in a state of schizophrenia where they are both guards and prisoners. And as a result they no longer have—having been lobotomized—the capacity to leave the prison they've made or even to see it as a prison." And then he went into his pocket, and he took out a seed for a tree, and he said, "This is a pine tree." And he put it in my hand. And he said, "Escape before it's too late."

WALLY: Gosh—

ANDRÉ: And you know, Wally, for two or three years now Chiquita and I have actually had this very unpleasant feeling that we really *should* get out. We really feel like Jews in Germany in the late thirties. Get out of here. Of course, the problem is where to go. Because it seems quite obvious that the whole world is going in the same direction. In fact, it seems to me quite possible that the nineteen-sixties represented the last burst of the human being before he was extinguished. And that this is the beginning of the rest of the future, now, and that from now on there will simply be all these robots walking around, feeling nothing, thinking nothing. And there will be nobody left almost to remind them that there once was a species called a human being, with feelings and thoughts. And that history and memory are right now being erased, and that soon no one will really remember that life existed on the planet.

WALLY: Uh-huh—

ANDRÉ: Now Gustav Björnstrand feels that there really is almost no hope, and that probably we'll be going back to a very savage, lawless, terrifying period. But the Findhorn people see it a little differently. They also feel that the world is getting darker and darker and colder and colder, but they also believe that it's a law of nature—because everything is balanced—that as one thing gets darker and colder, something else will get lighter and warmer. And it's their feeling that there will be these pockets of light springing up in different parts of the world, and that these will be in a way invisible planets on *this* planet and that, as we or the world grow colder, we will be able to take invisible space journeys to these different planets, refuel for what it is we have to do on the planet itself, and come back.

WALLY: Huh.

ANDRÉ: And you see, they believe that there have to be centers, now, where people can come and reconstruct a new future for the world. And when I was talking to Gustav Björnstrand, he was saying that these centers are actually growing up everywhere, and that what they're trying to do, which is also what Findhorn was trying to do, and in a way what I was trying to do—I mean these things can't be given a name—but in a way these are all attempts at creating a new kind of school or a new kind of monastery. And Björnstrand talked about the concept of—I think he calls it "re-serves"—islands of safety where history can be remembered and the human being can continue to function, in order to maintain the species through a Dark Age. In other words, we're talking about an underground, which did exist during the Dark Ages in a different way, among the mystical orders of the church. And the purpose of this underground is to find out how to preserve the light, life, the culture. How to keep things living. You see, I keep thinking that we need a new language, a language of the heart, a language, as in the Polish forest, where language wasn't needed—some kind of language between people that is a new kind of poetry, that is the poetry of the dancing bee, that tells us where the honey is. And I think that in order to create that language we're going to have to learn how you can go through a looking-glass into another kind of perception, in which you have that sense of being united to all things, and suddenly you understand everything.

Silence. WALLY *says nothing. The* WAITER *comes to the table, and* WALLY *and* ANDRÉ *order coffee.*

I mean, Wally, you see, there's this incredible building they built at Findhorn. And you see, they wanted to build a building that would seat about four or five hundred people. And the man who designed it had never designed anything in his life. He wrote children's books. And some people wanted it to be a sort of hall of meditation. And others wanted it to be a kind of lecture hall. But the psychic part of the community wanted it to serve another function as well, beause they wanted it to be a kind of spaceship which at night could rise up and let the UFOs know that this was a safe place to land and that they would find friends there. So the problem was, because it needed a kind of massive roof, was how to have a roof that would stay on the building and yet at the same time be able to fly up at night to meet the flying saucers. So the architect meditated and meditated and came up with the simple solution of not actually joining the roof to the building, which means that it should fall off, because they have great gales up in Northern Scotland. So to keep it from falling off he got beach stones, about this large, from the beach—or we did, because I worked on this building—all up and down the roof, just like that, touching, and the idea was that the energy that would go from stone to stone, you see, would be so strong that it would keep the roof down under any conditions, but at the same time if the roof needed to go up it would be light enough to go up. Well, it works, you see. Now, architects don't know *why* it works, and it *shouldn't* work, because it should fall off, but it works. It does work. The gales blow, and the roof should fall off, but it doesn't fall off.

WALLY: Yeah. Well, you see— Well, André, you know, if you want to know my *actual* response to all this—do you want to hear my actual response?

ANDRÉ: Yes!

WALLY: Well, André, I mean, my *actual* response—I mean, André, really—I'm just trying to survive—you know? I mean, I'm trying to earn a living, I'm trying to pay my rent and my bills. I mean, I live my life, I enjoy staying home with Debby, I'm reading Charlton Heston's autobiography, and that's that. (*Pause.*) I mean, occasionally, maybe, Debby and I will step outside and we'll go to a party or something, and if I can occasionally get my little talent together and write a play, well then that's wonderful, and I enjoy reading about other little plays that people have written, and reading the reviews of those plays and what people said about them, and what people said about what people said. And I mean, I have a list of errands and responsibilities that I keep in a notebook, and I enjoy going through my list and carrying out the responsibilities and doing the errands and then crossing them off my list. And I mean, I just don't know how anybody could enjoy anything *more* than I enjoy reading Charlton Heston's autobiography and, you know, getting up in the morning and having the cup of cold coffee that's been waiting for me all night *still there* for me to drink in the morning, and no cockroach or fly has died in it overnight—I'm just so *thrilled* when I get up, and I see that coffee there, just the way I want it, I just can't imagine enjoying something else any more than that. I mean, obviously if the cockroach—if there *is* a dead cockroach in it, then I just have a feeling of disappointment, and I'm sad. But I mean, I don't think I feel the need for anything more than all this. Whereas you seem to be saying that it's inconceivable that anybody could be having a meaningful life today, and everyone is totally destroyed, and we need to live in these out-

posts—But I mean, even for you, I just can't believe—
I mean, don't you find—isn't it pleasant just to get up
in the morning, and there's Chiquita, there are the
children, the *Times* is delivered, you can read it,
and—maybe you'll direct a play, maybe you *won't*
direct a play, but forget about the play that you may
or may not direct—why is it necessary to—why not
lean back and just *enjoy* these details? I mean, and
there would be a delicious cup of coffee, and a piece
of coffee cake. I mean, why is it necessary to have
more than this, or to even *think* about having more
than this? I mean, I don't *really* know what you're
talking about. I mean, I know what you're talking
about, but I don't *really* know what you're talking
about. And I mean, actually, even if I *did* feel the
way you do—you know, that there's no possibility for
happiness now—then, frankly, I *still* couldn't accept
the idea that the way to make life wonderful would
be to totally reject Western civilization and to fall
back into a kind of belief in some kind of weird something. I mean—I mean, I don't even know how to
begin talking about this, but I mean—I mean, you
know, in the Middle Ages, before the arrival of scientific thinking as we know it today, well, people could
believe *anything—anything* could be true—a statue of
the Virgin Mary *could* speak or bleed or whatever.
But the wonderful thing that happened was that
then in the development of science in the Western
world certain things *did* come slowly to be known
and understood. I mean, of *course* all ideas in science are constantly being revised—I mean, that's the
whole point—but we do at least know that the universe has *some* shape and order and that, you know,
trees do *not* turn into people or goddesses, and there

are very good reasons *why* they don't, and you can't just believe absolutely anything. And I mean, the things you're talking about—I mean, either the stones have the weight to hold down that roof, or they don't. And I mean, when you talk about things like that flag or the handprints—I mean, you seem constantly to be finding a significance in these things that to me are just *facts*. I mean, you found the handprints in the book, and they were three Andrés and one Antoine de Saint-Exupéry. And to me that is a coincidence. And the people who put that book together had their own reasons for putting it together. But to you it was significant, as if that book had been written forty years ago so that you would see it—as if it was planned for you in a way. I mean, really—I mean, André, let's say—I mean, if I get a fortune cookie in a Chinese restaurant, I mean, of *course* even *I* have a tendency—I mean, *you* know, I would hardly throw it out—I mean, I read it, I read it, and I—I just instinctively sort of—if it says something like—uh—a conversation with a dark-haired man will be very important for you, I mean, I just instinctively think, Well, who do I know who has dark hair, and did we have a conversation, and what did we talk about? In other words, I mean, I do tend to read it—but it's a joke, in my mind. I mean, in other words, there's something in me that makes me read it, and I instinctively interpret it as if it really were an omen of the future. But in my *conscious* opinion, which is so fundamental to my whole view of life—I mean, I would have to change totally, I think, to not have this opinion—in my *conscious* opinion, this is simply something that was written in the cookie factory several years ago and in no way refers to me. I mean, the fact that I got it—the man who wrote it did not know anything about me, couldn't have known anything about me. There's no way that this cookie could actually have anything to do with me. The fact that I've gotten it is basically a joke. And I mean, if I were planning to go on a trip on an airplane, and I got a fortune cookie that said "Don't go," I mean I admit I might feel a bit nervous for about one second, but in fact I would go, because I mean, that trip is going to be successful or unsuccessful based on the state of the airplane and the state of the pilot. And the cookie is in no position to know about that. And it's the same with any kind of prophesy or sign or omen. Because if you believe in omens, then that means that the universe—I can hardly begin to describe this—that somehow the future can send messages backward to the present. Which means that the future exists in some sense already in order to be able to send these messages. And it also means that things in the universe are there for a purpose, to give us messages. Whereas I believe that things in the universe are just there. They don't mean anything. I mean, if the turtle's egg falls out of the tree and splashes on the paving stones, it's just because that turtle was clumsy by accident. And to decide whether to send my ships off to war on the basis of that seems a big mistake to me.

ANDRÉ: Well, uh, what information *would* you send your ships to war on? Because if it's all meaningless, then what's the difference whether you accept the fortune cookie or the statistics of the Ford Foundation? It doesn't seem to matter.

WALLY: Well, the meaningless fact of the fortune cookie or the turtle's egg can't possibly have any relevance to the subject you're analyzing. Whereas a group of meaningless facts which are collected and interpreted in a scientific way may quite possibly *be* relevant. Because the great thing about scientific theories about things is that they're based on experiments that can be *repeated*.

The WAITER *serves coffee.*

ANDRÉ: Uh-huh. Uh-huh.

WALLY: I mean, if you're sending your ships to war, and you don't believe the current scientific opinions about the tides of the ocean, then you can repeat the experiments that everyone has done and see if you can come up with different results. Or you can try to show that those experiments are not the ones which should have been conducted.

ANDRÉ: Uh-huh. Mm-hmm. (*Long silence.*) Well, you know, the truth is, Wally, that in retrospect those things that I was involved in are all, in a way, disgusting to me. I mean, I look back on it, and, you know, really, the thought that I was playing with flags and so on—I mean, you know— Because, you see, *I* think what it means to be involved in those things in a way is that you've entered the unconscious, that you're in the world of the unconscious, and that to some extent your ego has gone, or your ego base has dissolved, and in that sense, I mean, you're in the underworld. And you can actually begin to think that you have the unconscious ability to make signs or omens happen, and you can get very excited by it because I guess you think you have some kind of power. And that's disturbing. I mean, you know, following omens and so on is probably just a way of letting ourselves off the hook so that we don't have to take individual responsibility for our own actions. After all, it's not easy for us to make our own decisions, because our knowledge of ourselves is too limited, and our ability to take what we feel and somehow develop it into concrete positive action for ourselves is too limited, so that rather than standing on our own feet and saying, "This is what I believe, this is what I want, this is what I need," we pretend we're following these omens or whatever. And I agree with you that that is frightening. I mean, and giving yourself over to the unconscious can leave you vulnerable to all sorts of very frightening manipulation. And in all the work that I was involved in, there was always that danger. And there was always that question of tampering with people's lives, because if I lead one of these workshops, then I do become partly a doctor and partly a therapist and partly a priest. And yet I'm *not* a doctor or a therapist or a priest. And already some of these new "monasteries" or whatever we've been talking about are becoming institutionalized, and I guess even in a way at times sort of fascistic, and there's a sort of self-satisfied elitist paranoia that grows up, a feeling of "them" and "us" that is very unsettling. I mean, some of these people can build up a kind of network of beliefs founded on signs from anywhere that proves without any question that they're absolutely right about everything. And you know, you sit around and have

dinner in some of these places, and everybody is talking with great knowledge about Atlantis or whatever
it is, and you know, you feel very strange if you don't
happen to have all this secret information. And then
they see all these significant coincidences in everything that happens. And that kind of self-contained,
self-ratifying certainty can lead to terrible conse-
quences, as we know. But the thing is, Wally, I think
it's the exaggerated worship of science that has led us
into this situation. I mean, science has been held up
to us as a magical force that would somehow solve
everything. Well, quite the contrary. It's done quite
the contrary. It's destroyed everything. So that is
really what has led to this very strong, deep reaction
against science that we're seeing now, just as the Nazi
demons that were released in the thirties in Germany
were probably a reaction against a certain oppressive
kind of knowledge and culture and rational thinking.
And so I agree that we're talking about something
potentially very dangerous. But modern science has
not been particularly *less* dangerous.

WALLY: Yeah. I know. That's all absolutely true. (*Pause.*)
You know, the truth is, I think I do know what *really*
disturbs me about the work that you've described—
and I don't even know if I can express it, André—but
somehow, if I've understood what you've been saying, it somehow seems that the whole point of the
work that you did in those workshops, when you get
right down to it and ask what it really was about—the
whole *point*, really, I think, was to enable the people
in the workshops, including yourself, to somehow sort
of strip away every scrap of *purposefulness* from certain selected moments. And the point of it was so

that you would then be able to experience somehow just *pure being*. In other words, you were trying to discover what it would be like to live for certain moments without having any particular thing that you were supposed to be doing. I mean, that was the purpose of these workshops, really. And I think I just simply object to that. I mean, I just don't think I accept the idea that there should *be* moments in which you're not trying to do anything. I think it's our nature to do things. I think we should do things. I think purposefulness is part of our ineradicable basic human structure. And to say that we ought to be able to live without it is like saying that a tree ought to be able to live without branches or roots; but actually, without branches or roots, it wouldn't be a tree. I mean, it would just be a log. Do you see what I'm saying?

ANDRÉ: Uh-huh.

WALLY: I mean, if I'm sitting at home and I have nothing to do, well, I naturally reach for a book. I mean, what would be so great about just sitting there and doing nothing? It seems absurd.

ANDRÉ: And if Debby is there?

WALLY: Well, that's the same thing. I mean, is there really such a thing as two people doing nothing but just simply being together? Would they simply then be "relating," to use the word we're always using? What would that mean? I mean, either we're going to have a conversation or we're going to carry out the garbage or we're going to do *something*, separately or together. Do you see what I'm saying? I mean, what does it mean to just simply sit there?

ANDRÉ: That makes you nervous.

WALLY: Well, why shouldn't it make me nervous? It just seems ridiculous to me.

ANDRÉ: Yeah. Uh-huh. Well that's interesting, Wally, because, you know, when I went to Ladakh—you know, that's on the border of China and Tibet—and stayed on a farm for a month—well, there, you know, when people come over in the evening for tea, nobody says anything. Unless there's something to say, but there almost never is. So they sit there and they drink their tea. And it doesn't seem to bother them.

WALLY: Uh-huh. Yeah.

Pause.

ANDRÉ: You see, Wally, the trouble with always being active and doing things is that it's quite possible to do all sorts of things and at the same time be completely dead inside. I mean, you're doing all these things, but are you doing them because you really feel an impulse to do them, or are you doing them mechanically, as we were saying before? Because I do believe that if you're just living mechanically, then you have to change your life. I mean, you know, when you're young, you go out on dates all the time, you go dance or something, you're floating free, and then one day you find yourself in a relationship, and suddenly everything freezes. And this can be true in your work as well. And I mean, as long as you're really alive inside, then of course there's no problem. I mean, you know, if you're living with someone in one little room, and there's a life going on between you and the person you're living with, well then, you know, a whole adventure can be going on right in that room. But there's always that danger that things can go dead. And then I think you really do have to kind of become a hobo or something, you know, like Kerouac, and go out on the road. I really believe that. I mean, it's not that wonderful to spend your life on the road. I mean, my own overwhelming preference is to stay in that room if you can! Now, of course, if you live with somebody for a long time, people are constantly saying, "Well, of course it's not as great as it used to be, but that's only natural. The first blush of a romance goes, you know, and that's the way it has to be." Now, I totally disagree with that. But I do think you have to constantly ask yourself the question, with total frankness, is your marriage still a marriage? Is the sacramental element still there? Just as you have to ask about the sacramental element of your work—is it still there? And I mean, it's a very frightening thing to have to realize suddenly that, my God, I thought I was living my life, but in fact I haven't been a human being. I've been a performer. I haven't been living. I've been acting. I've acted the role of the father. I've acted the role of the husband. I've acted the role of the friend. I've acted the role of the writer or director or whatever. I've lived in the same room with this person, but I haven't really seen them. I haven't really heard them. I haven't really been with them.

WALLY: I know what you mean. Sometimes people are just existing side by side. I mean, the other—the other person's face could just turn into a great wolf's face for seconds, and it just wouldn't be noticed.

ANDRÉ: It wouldn't be noticed, no. It wouldn't be noticed. I mean, Wally, when I was in Israel a little while ago—I mean, I have this picture of Chiquita that I always carry with me, and it was taken when she was about twenty-six or something, and it's in summer, and she's stretched out on a terrace in this sort of old-fashioned long skirt that's kind of pulled up, and she's slim and sensual and beautiful, and I've always looked at that picture, and I've always thought about just how sexy she looks. And this year in Israel I looked at the picture, and I realized that the face in the picture was the saddest face in the world. That girl at that time was lost, just so sad and so alone. And I've been carrying this picture for years, and not ever really seeing what it is, you know. I just had never really looked at the picture. And you see, at a certain point I just simply realized that I had gone for a good eighteen years unable to feel except in the most extreme situations. And I realized that in fact every day of one's life is made up of a thousand constantly shifting feelings. I mean, I always knew this in the theater. That was precisely my conception of what a play was. But I didn't know it in my life. And I didn't really accept the fact that I am a creature who wants to die of love for my daughter one moment, and then the next moment I want to lock her in the cookie jar. I mean, to some extent I still had the ability to live in my work—that was why I was such a work junkie. That was why I felt that every play I did was a matter of my life and death. But in my real life, I was dead. I was a robot. I mean, my life with Chiquita has always been the most important thing in the world to me. But then, it was frozen, because I was afraid that if I allowed myself to feel anything, I'd destroy everything. I mean, Wally, at that time I didn't even allow myself to feel angry or annoyed! I mean, *today*, you know, well, Nicolas, Marina, and Chiquita all day long, as people do, will do things that annoy me or say things that annoy me. And *today* I get annoyed. And they say, "Why are you annoyed?" And I say, "Because you're annoying," you know. And when I allowed myself to consider the possibility of not spending the rest of my life with Chiquita, I realized that what I wanted most in life was to always be with her. But at that time, Wally, I hadn't learned what it would be like to let yourself react to another person, to follow your impulses with another person from moment to moment along a chain of feeling that can change from one second to the next. And you see, if you can't react to another person, then there's no possibility of action or interaction, and if there isn't, then I don't really know what the word "love" means except duty, obligation, sentimentality, fear. . . . (*Pause.*) I mean, I don't know about you, Wally, but I just had to put myself into a kind of training program to learn how to be a human being. I mean, what did I feel about anything? I didn't know. What kind of things did I like? What kind of people did I really want to be with? You know. And the only way I could think of to find out was to just cut out all the noise around me and stop performing for a few moments and just listen to what was inside me. I think there comes a time when you need to do that. Now maybe in order to do it, you have to go to the Sahara, and maybe you can do it at home. But you need to cut out the noise.

WALLY: Yeah. Of course, personally, I don't usually like those quiet moments, you know. I really don't. I mean, I don't know if it's that Freudian thing or what—I mean, a fear of unconscious impulses or my own aggression or—I mean, if things get too quiet, you know, and as we were saying, I find myself just sitting there, whether I'm by myself, or I'm with somebody else, well, I just have this feeling of, My God, I'm going to be *revealed*. I mean, I'm adequate to do any sort of task, you know, but I'm not adequate just to *be* a human being. I mean, I'm not— you know, I mean, if I'm just *trapped* there and I'm not allowed to *do* things, but I just—all I can do is just be there—I—I will fail. In other words, I can pass any other test and get an "A" if I put in the required effort, but I don't have a clue how to pass *this* test. Of course, this *isn't* really a test, but I *see* it as a test, and I feel I'm going to fail it. I mean, it's really scary. I just feel totally at sea. I mean—

ANDRÉ: I mean, I can imagine a life, Wally, in which each day would become an incredible, monumental creative task—a life in which everybody would just go with their impulses, all day long—they would just be themselves every moment, with others. And we're not necessarily up to it. I mean, if you felt like walking out on the person you live with, you'd walk out. Then if you felt like it you'd come back. But meanwhile the other person would have reacted to your walking out. It would be a life of such feeling. In a way, it would be intoxicating. And I mean, what was amazing in the workshops I led was how quickly people seemed to fall into enthusiasm, celebration, joy, wonder, abandon, wildness, tenderness. And could we stand to live like that? I mean, maybe we're just simply afraid of living. Or maybe what we're really afraid of is thinking about a kind of existence that we've lost, which if we were to remember would make us give up everything.

WALLY: I think it's that moment of contact with another person. That's what scares us. That moment of being face to face with another person. I mean, you wouldn't think it would be so frightening. It's strange that we find it so frightening.

ANDRÉ: Well, it isn't that strange. After all, it isn't really that strange, Wally. I mean, after all, there are some pretty good reasons for being frightened, because first of all a human being is a dangerous and complex creature. I mean, really, if you start living each moment—Christ, that's quite a challenge. I mean, if you really reach out and you're really in touch with the other person—well, that really is something to strive for, I think—I really do.

WALLY: It's just so pathetic if one doesn't do that.

ANDRÉ: Absolutely. It's just nothing. I mean, at least attempt it—even if you can't make it, attempt it—even if you're going blind, do some kind of exercises for your eyes or, you know, something. But of course there's a problem, because the closer you come, I

think, to another human being, the more really completely mysterious that person becomes, and the
more unreachable. You know, you have to reach out
to that person, you have to go back and forth with
them, and you have to relate, and yet—you're relating
to a ghost. Or something. I don't know. Because
we're ghosts. *We're* phantoms. Who are we?

WALLY: Right.

ANDRÉ: And that's to face, to confront the fact that you're
completely alone, and to accept that you're alone is
to accept death.

WALLY: You mean, because somehow when you *are* alone
you're alone *with death*. Nothing's obstructing your
view of it, or something like that.

ANDRÉ: Right.

WALLY: If I understood it correctly, I think Heidegger said
that if you were to experience your own being to the
full, you would be experiencing the decay of that
being toward death as part of your experience.

ANDRÉ (*pause*): Yes. You know, in the sexual act there's
that moment of complete forgetting which is so incredible, and in the next moment you start to think
about things—work on the play, what you've got to
do tomorrow. I don't know if this is true of you, but I
think it must be quite common. The world comes in
quite fast. Now, that may be because we don't have
the courage to stay in that place of forgetting, because that is again close to death. Like people who

are afraid to go to sleep. In other words, you inter-relate, and you don't know what the next moment will bring. And to not know what the next moment will bring, I think, brings you closer to a perception of death. So that, paradoxically, the closer you get to living, in the sense of relating constantly, I guess the closer you get to this thing that we're most afraid of.

WALLY: Yeah.

ANDRÉ: You see, I think that's why people have affairs. I mean, you know, in the theater, if you get good reviews you feel for a moment that you've got your hands on something. You know what I mean? It's a good feeling. But then that feeling goes very quickly. And once again you don't know quite what will happen next, what you should do. Well, have an affair and up to a certain point you can really feel you're on firm ground. There is a sexual conquest to be made. There are different questions: does she enjoy the ears being nibbled? how intensely can you talk about Schopenhauer at an elegant French restaurant, or whatever nonsense it is. It's all I think to give you the semblance that there's firm earth. But have a real relationship with a person that goes on for years—well, that's completely unpredictable. Then, you've cut off all your ties to the land, and you're sailing into the unknown, into uncharted seas. And I mean, people hang on to these images of father, mother, husband, wife, again, for the same reason, because they seem to provide some firm ground. But there's no wife there. What does that mean? A wife. A husband. A son. A baby holds your hands, and then suddenly there's this huge man lifting you off the ground, and then he's gone. Where's that son? You know?

WALLY: Yeah.

WALLY *looks up. The restaurant is empty. The* WAITER *approaches. Music. Erik Satie's* Gymnopédie #1 *plays under* WALLY's *voice.*

(*Voice-over*) All the other customers seemed to have left hours ago. We got the bill, and André paid for our dinner.

WALLY *is outside, riding in a taxi.*

(*Voice-over*) I treated myself to a taxi.

WALLY *looks out the taxi window.*

I rode home through the city streets. There wasn't a street—there wasn't a building—that wasn't connected to some memory in my mind. There, I was buying a suit with my father. There, I was having an ice cream soda after school.

The city streets rush by.

When I finally came in, Debby was home from work, and I told her everything about my dinner with André.

OTHER GROVE PRESS DRAMA AND THEATER PAPERBACKS

B415   ARDEN, JOHN / John Arden Plays: One (Serjeant Musgrave's Dance, The Workhouse Donkey, Armstrong's Last Goodnight) / $4.95

E610   ARRABAL, FERNANDO / And They Put Handcuffs on the Flowers / $1.95

E611   ARRABAL, FERNANDO / Garden of Delights / $2.95

E521   ARRABAL, FERNANDO / Guernica and Other Plays (The Labyrinth, The Tricycle, Picnic on the Battlefield) / $4.95

B423   AYCKBOURN, ALAN / Absurd Person Singular, Absent Friends, Bedroom Farce: Three Plays / $3.95

E425   BARAKA, IMAMU AMIRI (LeRoi Jones) / The Baptism and The Toilet: Two Plays / $3.95 [See also Grove Press Modern Drama, John Lahr, ed., E633 / $5.95]

E670   BARAKA, IMAMU AMIRI (LeRoi Jones) / The System of Dante's Hell, The Dead Lecturer and Tales / $4.95

E471   BECKETT, SAMUEL / Cascando and Other Short Dramatic Pieces (Words and Music, Eh Joe, Play, Come and Go, Film) / $3.95

E96   BECKETT, SAMUEL / Endgame / $2.45

E680   BECKETT, SAMUEL / Ends and Odds / $1.95

E502   BECKETT, SAMUEL / Film, A Film Script / $1.95

E623   BECKETT, SAMUEL / First Love and Other Shorts / $1.95

E318   BECKETT, SAMUEL / Happy Days / $2.95

E692   BECKETT, SAMUEL / I Can't Go On; I'll Go On / $6.95

E226   BECKETT, SAMUEL / Krapp's Last Tape and Other Dramatic Pieces (All That Fall, Embers [a Play for Radio], Acts Without Words I and II [mimes]) / $3.95

E777   BECKETT, SAMUEL / Rockaby and Other Works / $3.95

E33   BECKETT, SAMUEL / Waiting for Godot / $2.95

B411   BEHAN, BRENDAN / The Complete Plays (The Hostage, The Quare Fellow, Richard's Cork Leg, Three One Act Plays for Radio) / $4.95

B60	BRECHT, BERTOLT / Baal, A Man's A Man, The Elephant Calf / $1.95 [See also Seven Plays by Bertolt Brecht, GP248 / $12.50 and The Jewish Wife and Other Short Plays, B80 / $1.95]
B312	BRECHT, BERTOLT / The Caucasian Chalk Circle / $1.95
B119	BRECHT, BERTOLT / Edward II: A Chronicle Play / $1.95
B120	BRECHT, BERTOLT / Galileo / $1.95 [See also Seven Plays by Bertolt Brecht, GP248 / $12.50]
B117	BRECHT, BERTOLT / The Good Woman of Setzuan / $1.95 [See also Seven Plays by Bertolt Brecht, GP248 / $12.50]
B80	BRECHT, BERTOLT / The Jewish Wife and Other Short Plays (In Search of Justice, The Informer, The Elephant Calf, The Measures Taken, The Exception and the Rule, Salzburg Dance of Death) / $1.95
B89	BRECHT, BERTOLT / The Jungle of Cities and Other Plays (Drums in the Night, Roundheads and Peakheads) / $3.95
B129	BRECHT, BERTOLT / Manual of Piety / $2.45
B414	BRECHT, BERTOLT / The Mother / $2.95
B108	BRECHT, BERTOLT / Mother Courage and Her Children / $1.95
B333	BRECHT, BERTOLT / The Threepenny Opera / $1.95
B193	BULGAKOV, MIKHAIL / Heart of a Dog / $2.95
B147	BULGAKOV, MIKHAIL / The Master and Margarita / $3.95
E773	CLURMAN, HAROLD / Nine Plays of the Modern Theater (Waiting for Godot by Samuel Beckett, The Visit by Friedrich Dürrenmatt, Tango by Slawomir Mrozek, The Caucasian Chalk Circle by Bertolt Brecht, The Balcony by Jean Genet, Rhinoceros by Eugène Ionesco, American Buffalo by David Mamet, The Birthday Party by Harold Pinter, and Rosencrantz and Guildenstern Are Dead by Tom Stoppard) / $11.95
B459	COWARD, NOEL / Plays: One (Hay Fever, The Vortex, Fallen Angels, Easy Virtue) / $6.50
B460	COWARD, NOEL / Plays: Two (Private Lives, Bitter-Sweet, The Marquise, Post Mortem) / $6.50
B461	COWARD, NOEL / Plays: Three (Design for Living, Cavalcade, Conversation Piece, and three plays from Tonight at 8:30: Hands Across the Sea, Still Life, Fumed Oak) / $6.50

E485   IONESCO, EUGENE / A Stroll in the Air and Frenzy for Two or More: Two Plays / $2.45

E496   JARRY, ALFRED / The Ubu Plays (Ubu Rex, Ubu Cuckolded, Ubu Enchained) / $4.95

E633   LAHR, JOHN, ed. / Grove Press Modern Drama (The Toilet by Imamu Amiri Baraka [LeRoi Jones], The Caucasian Chalk Circle by Bertolt Brecht, The White House Murder Case by Jules Feiffer, The Blacks by Jean Genet, Rhinoceros by Eugene Ionesco, Tango by Slawomir Mrozek) / $5.95

E697   MAMET, DAVID / American Buffalo / $3.95

E778   MAMET, DAVID / Lakeboat / $4.95

E709   MAMET, DAVID / A Life in the Theatre / $3.95

E728   MAMET, DAVID / Reunion and Dark Pony: Two Plays / $2.95

E712   MAMET, DAVID / Sexual Perversity in Chicago and The Duck Variations: Two Plays / $3.95

E716   MAMET, DAVID / The Water Engine and Mr. Happiness: Two Plays / $3.95

B107   MOON, SAMUEL, ed. / One Act: Eleven Short Plays of the Modern Theater (Miss Julie by August Strindberg, Purgatory by William Butler Yeats, The Man With the Flower in His Mouth by Luigi Pirandello, Pullman Car Hiawatha by Thornton Wilder, Hello Out There by William Saroyan, 27 Wagons Full of Cotton by Tennessee Williams, Bedtime Story by Sean O'Casey, Cecile by Jean Anouilh, This Music Crept By Me Upon the Waters by Archibald MacLeish, A Memory of Two Mondays by Arthur Miller, The Chairs by Eugene Ionesco) / $3.95

E789   MROZEK, SLAWOMIR / Striptease, Tango, Vatzlav: Three Plays / $6.95

E433   MROZEK, SLAWOMIR / Tango / $3.95

E568   MROZEK, SLAWOMIR / Vatzlav / $1.95

E650   NICHOLS, PETER / The National Health / $3.95

B429   ODETS, CLIFFORD / Six Plays of Clifford Odets (Waiting for Lefty, Awake and Sing, Golden Boy, Rocket to the Moon, Till the Day I Die, Paradise Lost) / $5.95

WESTMAR COLLEGE LIBRARY

E684   STOPPARD, TOM / Dirty Linen and New-Found-Land: Two Plays / $2.95

E703   STOPPARD, TOM / Every Good Boy Deserves Favor and The Professional Foul: Two Plays / $3.95

E626   STOPPARD, TOM / Jumpers / $2.95

E726   STOPPARD, TOM / Night and Day / $3.95

E489   STOPPARD, TOM / The Real Inspector Hound and After Magritte: Two Plays / $3.95

B319   STOPPARD, TOM / Rosencrantz and Guildenstern Are Dead / $2.25

E661   STOPPARD, TOM / Travesties / $2.95

E62   WALEY, ARTHUR, tr. and ed. / The No Plays of Japan / $5.95

CRITICAL STUDIES

E127   ARTAUD, ANTONIN / The Theater and Its Double / $3.95

E743   BENTLEY, ERIC / The Brecht Commentaries / $9.50

E441   COHN, RUBY, ed. / Casebook on Waiting for Godot / $4.95

E603   HARRISON, PAUL CARTER / The Drama of Nommo: Black Theater in the African Continuum / $2.45

E695   HAYMAN, RONALD / How To Read A Play / $2.95

E387   IONESCO, EUGENE / Notes and Counternotes: Writings on the Theater / $3.95

GROVE PRESS, INC., 196 West Houston St., New York, N.Y. 10014